Advance Praise for
for Armcha

"Edwards was not an armchair kind of guy (and he would have been unhappy about some of the cartoons), but James Byrd has done a great job of clearly presenting what there is to like about Edwards and his theology."

—George M. Marsden, author of
A Short Life of Jonathan Edwards

"Many thanks to Professor Byrd for this graceful and witty introduction to the thought of one whose work deserves a much greater hearing outside the world of conservative Calvinism. Just right for general readers, this lively book will inform and delight. You'd better watch out, though, for its graceful prose conveys the power to charm unwary readers out of their armchairs and into the deep ocean of Edwards' theological art."

—Douglas A. Sweeney, Associate Professor
of Church History, Trinity Evangelical Divinity School

Jonathan Edwards for Armchair Theologians

Also Available in the Armchair Series

12,71

Jonathan Edwards
for Armchair Theologians

JAMES P. BYRD

ILLUSTRATIONS BY RON HILL

Westminster John Knox Press
LOUISVILLE • LONDON

Scripture quotations from the New Revised Standard Version of the
Bible are copyright © 1989 by the Division of Christian Education
of the National Council of the Churches of Christ in the U.S.A. and
are used by permission.

Book design by Sharon Adams
Cover design by Jennifer K. Cox
Cover illustration by Ron Hill

First edition
Published by Westminster John Knox Press
Louisville, Kentucky

This book is printed on acid-free paper that meets the American
National Standards Institute Z39.48 standard.

PRINTED IN THE UNITED STATES OF AMERICA

08 09 10 11 12 13 14 15 16 17 — 10 9 8 7 6 5 4 3 2 1

Library of Congress Cataloging-in-Publication Data

Byrd, James P.
   Jonathan Edwards for armchair theologians / James P. Byrd ;
illustrations by Ron Hill.— 1st ed.
       p. cm.
   Includes bibliographical references (p.   ) and index.
   ISBN 978-0-664-23199-6 (alk. paper)
   1. Edwards, Jonathan, 1703–1758. I. Title.

BX7260.E3B97 2008
230'.58092—dc22
                                        2008008477

To
Richard F. Wilson

Contents

Acknowledgments   ix

Introduction   xi

1. The Young Edwards: Exploring Divine Beauty (Even in Spiders)   1

2. An Affection for Revival   35

3. Exodus from Northampton   61

4. Freedom of the Will?   77

5. Original Sin   103

6. Creation and True Virtue   127

7. A Legacy Begun: The Edwards Ethos   147

Notes   175

For Further Reading   183

Index   191

Acknowledgments

I am grateful for the advice of friends and colleagues who have made this a much better book than it would have been otherwise. Kenneth P. Minkema and Douglas A. Sweeney read chapter drafts and offered many valuable suggestions. I greatly appreciated their gracious willingness to share their expertise on Jonathan Edwards. Matthew McCullough, a graduate student in American religious history at Vanderbilt, was incredibly helpful throughout the writing process, reading drafts, correcting mistakes, and offering much good advice. I would not have imagined writing this book had I not received excellent introductions to Edwards through the work of great teachers, especially John Fitzmier and Bradley Longfield. My colleagues at Vanderbilt have been wonderfully supportive of my work on this book. I learned much from conversations with Victor Anderson, Patout Burns, Paul DeHart, Kathleen Flake, Bill Hook, James Hudnut-Beumler, Paul Lim, John McClure, Douglas Meeks, and Ted Smith. I am also thankful that Vanderbilt has given me the opportunity to work with outstanding students in seminars on American revivals, theology in America, and even a course on Jonathan Edwards. I would probably not have finished this book on time without the excellent work of my administrative colleague, Marie McEntire. I owe her many thanks. It was a privilege to work with Nicole Smith Murphy at Westminster John Knox Press. She was an enthusiastic

Acknowledgments

reader and editor; her suggestions improved the book in many ways. Most of all I am grateful to my wife, Karen M. Byrd, and our daughters, Olivia and Caroline. They allowed me the space and time to complete this book. But, more importantly, they inspire me in everything I do. I am pleased to dedicate this book to Richard F. Wilson—teacher, preacher, theologian (and sometimes poet).

James P. Byrd
Nashville, TN
April 2008

INTRODUCTION

Let me guess: your first encounter with Jonathan Edwards was disturbing. For decades high school English teachers have terrorized their students by requiring them to read "Sinners in the Hands of an Angry God," the sermon that made Edwards infamous and secured his reputation as an expert on the horrors of hell. If that was your experience, it probably wasn't your most horrifying experience in high school (for me, that was the junior prom). Still, if you did encounter Edwards in first-period English class, he probably got your attention. Just about anyone would have to flinch at Edwards's description of God as an irate archer who aims his "arrow at your heart, and strains the bow," threatening to release it at any moment.[1] So this is Jonathan Edwards, many teenagers have thought to themselves as they skimmed these terrifying lines and wondered if they would be on the test. If that was not your experience, good. You won't have to purge that dreadful image of Edwards from your mind. You'll be open to explore the impressive expression of Edwards's life and thought—a world much more complex and beautiful than "Sinners." (Though, admittedly, "Sinners" is not without its own complexity, even a kind of beauty.) For those of you who have read only "Sinners," never fear—or at least don't fear Edwards. Though first impressions can be hard to overcome, I invite you to try. In this book there's much more to look forward to than hellfire images of arrows aimed at our hearts and spiders hanging over raging flames—though there will be more spiders, lots of spiders. And much more.

My purpose in this book is to introduce the general reader to Edwards's thought and influence. So if you still associate Edwards with hell, this book invites to you reacquaint yourself with him, perhaps with a more congenial and thorough introduction. You'll discover in these pages a preacher whose pulpit helped launch the widespread revivals that historians call the Great Awakening—arguably the most important mass social movement in colonial America prior to the Revolutionary War. These and later revivals empowered the explosion of Baptist and Methodist growth throughout the United States and gave us numerous influential leaders from Edwards and George Whitefield to Charles Finney, Dwight Moody, and Billy Graham. You will meet here also America's first prominent theologian and arguably its greatest theologian. If philosophy is your interest, you will find in Edwards the most profound philosophical writing coming out of colonial America, some of it written on the unpredictable frontier, where

Introduction

Edwards's deep thoughts were interspersed with the fear of attack from the French and their Native American allies. And you will also find that Edwards was among the great writers in early America. There is indeed good reason why "Sinners in the Hands of an Angry God" continues to be published in literary anthologies—for all its hellacious images, it's good writing. Finally, the ethicists among us may appreciate Edwards's explanation of the intimate relationship between the virtuous life, faith, and God's purpose in creating the world.

Edwards continues to fascinate scholars in departments that span an entire university campus. For so many—historians, philosophers, ethicists, theologians, literary specialists—Edwards remains interesting because the questions he pondered in his time are dilemmas that remain vital today. Among the many issues he sought to address are: What is freedom? Do we control our own destinies, and if so, is God in control of the world? Why do sin and evil affect us all? Does God need humanity? If so, is the all-powerful God dependent on frail humans? And if God doesn't need us, then why were we created? What is our place in the divine plan for the universe? And how should modern people make sense of the relationship between spiritual experience and rational thought?

This final question—the relationship between faith and reason—was perhaps most critical for Edwards. Born in a Puritan family and faithful to its traditional Calvinist theological beliefs, Edwards lived in a rapidly changing world. He grew up during the dawning of the Enlightenment, the age of reason, when many cutting-edge thinkers rejected Edwards's Calvinist view of the world. To truly understand Edwards, therefore, one must see how he had to come to terms with two worldviews that clashed before his eyes: the Puritan world of his past and the Enlightenment world that promised to dominate America's future. Though both traditions profoundly shaped the contours of American religion in years to come, the tension between the two was as strong in Edwards's day as it is in ours. And Jonathan Edwards was among the first brilliant thinkers to wrestle with its implications. As you read this book, wrestle along with Edwards. Along the way, I invite you to appreciate the crises he perceived and to ponder the solutions he devised.

CHAPTER ONE

The Young Edwards
Exploring Divine Beauty
(Even in Spiders)

Imagine meeting the young Jonathan Edwards. What would it have been like to know him as a child, growing up with his father, mother, and sisters in East Windsor, Connecticut?

Would we have appreciated the opportunity of studying with a teenage Edwards at Yale? Would we have recognized his budding brilliance? Or if we were parishioners in his first pastorate, a Presbyterian church in New York City, would we have had any clue that our pastor would become perhaps the greatest theologian in American history? Actually, if we had known Edwards in any of these places, we might not have predicted what the future would hold, but we probably would have realized quickly that Edwards was an intense, serious young man who did not care for casual conversation. Physically, the young Edwards was gaunt and lanky: tall (likely a trait inherited from his mother) and quite thin (a result of severe dietary restrictions he forced on himself so that he could spend less time eating and more time studying and praying).

His personality might not have won us over. First, he worried about his salvation to the point of near obsession. From his earliest years he was deeply anxious about the state of his soul and fully expected that he might go to hell, even after he had committed himself to ministry. Second, not only was Jonathan the poster child for Puritan anxiety, his social skills were questionable from the start. Though he was at the top of his college class, he was not popular at all with his peers. Several of his fellow students despised him for his aloof, serious disposition, and he in turn criticized them for their juvenile behavior that interrupted his study. He often came across as a young man who was out of place in the company of other young men. Youth, it seems, did not suit Edwards. But his youthful experiences set the patterns that would guide his considerable influence later on.

Had we given Edwards a chance, however, we assuredly would have noticed his dazzling intellect and his insatiable curiosity. He immersed himself in the many forms of new knowledge that erupted in the eighteenth-century enlightened age. He became fascinated with English philosopher John Locke's new theories on how our minds process ideas, beginning with the perceptions of our senses, and the groundbreaking ideas of English mathematician and physicist Isaac Newton. The young Edwards read it all, or at least all he could find while living far from the intellectual centers of the European Enlightenment. If an important book made its way across the Atlantic and was within Jonathan's reach, he likely devoured it. Despite his broad interests, however, Edwards did not view new ideas as mere novelties to be enjoyed; they were tools to be used to understand better the nature of God's universe and particularly God's relationship to humanity. So while he read enthusiastically in natural science (called "natural philosophy" in his day) and exercised scientific skills to explore the mysteries of the natural world, these exercises served religious purposes. And while he read the latest in European and British writings on physics, moral philosophy, and the nature of human knowledge, he used these new insights to defend the theology of his Puritan heritage against modern challenges. Intellectually, Edwards always remained faithful to his Calvinist roots and Puritan ethos.

Beginnings

It was probably a foregone conclusion soon after he was born in October, 1703, that Jonathan Edwards would grow up to become a minister. His father, Timothy Edwards, was himself a pastor, and Edwards's mother, Esther Stoddard Edwards, was the daughter of a renowned minister in Northampton, Massachusetts—the famous Solomon Stoddard. Together, Timothy and Esther Edwards had eleven (eleven!) children, but Jonathan was the only boy. And since female ministers were unheard of in colonial New England, Jonathan was the only one who could continue the ministerial heritage on both sides of the Edwards-Stoddard household. This is not to say that Edwards's faith and ministry lacked female influences. Far from it. With his mother and ten sisters, Jonathan and his father were grossly outnumbered at home! More importantly, Jonathan's mother, Esther, was well known and respected for her gifts as a teacher and for her spiritual insights. Jonathan grew up watching his mother teach in their home—both children and adults. Women from the church regularly joined her for conversations on religious topics, meetings that she led for many years. Through his mother and his sisters, Jonathan had powerful examples of female piety all around him. As a result, when Jonathan

later wrote about revivalism and religious experiences, he often used female examples.[1]

The influence of Jonathan's father was at least as strong. When Jonathan was nine years old, it was his father's revival preaching that stirred his interest in salvation and ignited his anxiety about his status before God. At this point young Jonathan prayed five times each day, devoting himself to seeking God's will. He joined with other boys in covert prayer meetings. He and his friends "built a booth in a swamp, in a very secret and retired place, for a place of prayer."[2] Spirituality was apparently a kind of adventure for Edwards. If so, he was not unique in the eighteenth century. Across the Atlantic, John Wesley and his brother, Charles, would join their friends in forming a "holy club," which planted the seeds for the Methodist movement. As in the case of the young Wesleys, youthful prayer meetings did not completely ease the young Edwards's mind about his eternal situation. His episodes of religious excitement would be followed by depressed periods in which he doubted his own sincerity. Writing later in his *Personal Narrative*, which is a combination autobiographical statement and guide to spirituality, Edwards recalled that his boyhood religious "affections seemed to be lively" at times, but also "easily moved"—"in the process of time, my convictions and affections wore off," and he lapsed back into sin.[3] Later, in his *Religious Affections*, Edwards would compose a list of tests to determine whether religious feelings were legitimate. He realized that his boyhood affections would have failed these tests, in part because of their inconsistency.

As the family's only male child in a society led mostly by men, Jonathan received special attention from his father, who groomed him for ministry by training him in the true study of conversion—a deeply serious intellectual discipline

in Puritan culture. And in a culture that was serious about conversion, Jonathan's father was more serious than most. Timothy Edwards spent countless hours dissecting the conversion experiences of his parishioners, attempting to discern whether they were truly legitimate. This was serious business for Puritans, because they knew that Satan could generate false religious experiences and deceive the unsuspecting churchgoer into hell. From his father, therefore, Jonathan learned the mechanics of conversion.[4]

Jonathan also learned from his father that a ministerial career was not only eternally vital, it also carried a lot of earthly prestige. In contrast to today, when medicine and law are most lauded, ministers in Edwards's day were the most respected men in town. They were typically intellectuals, more educated than their peers, and they earned salaries that reflected their respected position.

To appreciate the important role of the minister in colonial New England we need to consider the power of the Puritan preaching. Today many mainline Protestants think of preaching as a form of religious communication, delivered in the church by a minister, usually once a week, with most sermons lasting no longer than thirty minutes. With this view of preaching in mind, imagine what it was like in Puritan New England, where ministers typically preached three times each week, with each sermon lasting up to two hours. Even the most devout churchgoers today probably spend less time in worship than reading newspapers, watching television and listening to the radio. But in Puritan New England, preaching served many of the purposes that we find in the media and in other social gatherings. Considered in today's terms, the Puritan sermon was more dominant than any single form of communication now, including television and the Internet. Puritans looked to the sermon for trustworthy instruction on politics, culture, and the news of the day. There were special sermons for nearly all kinds of occasions. Aside from weekly worship, ministers preached on election days, thanksgiving days, and fast days. There were artillery sermons to inspire soldiers on their way to the battlefield, and Puritans even attended execution sermons that warned of judgment and pleaded for repentance in the shadow of the gallows. The preacher, therefore, was amazingly authoritative not only for the church, but for the town as well.[5] That was the level of authority that young Jonathan observed from his father and grandfather in the pulpit, and that was the kind of authority and respect that Edwards later expected from his own parishioners. As we will observe, the mature Jonathan Edwards would face disappointments that the young Edwards never imagined.

With this optimistic view of ministry in mind, Edwards

began his formal preparation at age thirteen by attending
the Collegiate School of Connecticut in its Wethersfield
campus, and then three years later moved to New Haven
after the school had been reorganized as Yale College. In
its formative stages, Yale was to be the conservative alternative to Harvard, which many New Englanders believed
had drifted in a theologically liberal direction far from its
Puritan beginnings.

Jonathan's college years were intellectually fantastic and socially wretched. He distinguished himself in his studies. He became the valedictorian of his class, in part because he was all work and no play—unlike some of his fellow students who played cards, cursed, hung out all hours "night walking" and occasionally engaged in petty vandalism. Jonathan was appalled. He chastised his classmates for their behavior and reported their activities to school authorities. He wasn't popular with his classmates, but he didn't much care. There were too many books to read! However, Jonathan continued to struggle with his spiritual anxieties and they sometimes left him feeling miserable and nearly hopeless.[6]

A Biblical Standard of Behavior

By age nineteen, while he was working on his MA at Yale, Edwards became supply pastor of a Presbyterian congregation in New York City. During this time he started working on several notebooks, including his now invaluable

"Miscellanies," in which he recorded reflections on a variety of topics. He served in New York for eight months and was continually amazed by the wonders of the big city. For the first time, this country boy from New England came into contact with a variety of cultures and religions. One of Edwards's neighbors, for instance, was a Jewish man whom Edwards later called, interestingly, "the devoutest person" that he ever encountered.[7]

During this first ministerial appointment, the nineteen-year-old Edwards, continuing to struggle with his faith, yearned for any examples of devout piety he could find. His anxieties about the state of his soul had not subsided, and Edwards dealt with these anxieties by starting a diary—a long-held Puritan tradition. Puritans wrote diaries almost as much as they read Scripture, as they would use their diaries to measure themselves against the standards they found in the Bible.

In his diary, especially as compared to diaries written by his contemporaries, Edwards reveals much about how he thought of his place in the world. Consider another well-known diary from that time: that of Benjamin Franklin. Franklin and Edwards were brilliant thinkers who engaged modern ways of thinking, but they did so in very different ways. While Edwards became a master theologian in the Reformed tradition, Franklin became a deist who only lightly considered theology and focused on more "practical" intellectual pursuits, such as science and politics. Yet the two both had an introspective gene: both kept diaries and evaluated themselves and their behavior against particular standards. Franklin and Edwards often agreed on basic principles for living a good life, but they usually disagreed on why one ought to live by certain standards in the first place! For instance, consider Franklin's great character Poor Richard and his famous advice: "Early to bed and

early to rise, makes a man healthy, wealthy, and wise."
Compare this with the reason Edwards gave for being an
early riser: because "Christ has recommended rising early
in the morning, by his rising from the grave very early."[8]
What a marvelous example of how totally Edwards framed
his mind in biblical terms, even down to the smallest detail
of life! While both Franklin and Edwards valued getting a
jump start on the day, Franklin did so for practical reasons
(early rising supports good health and wisdom, not to
mention profitability) while Edwards did so for biblical reasons (rising early was a small way to commemorate the res-
urrection).

From his diary, Edwards drew up a list of rules for life
that he recorded in a notebook titled "Resolutions."
And, like Franklin, Edwards kept track of how well he followed the resolutions. Always precise, Edwards vowed to
work like a spiritually focused accountant, keeping a

monthly tally of violations of the resolutions. His plan was to use this data on degeneracy to calculate his annual rate of sin.[9]

Edwards started this list of resolutions about the same time that he started his diary, when he was about nineteen. Not surprisingly, Edwards's resolutions included many religious convictions, and he probably spent lots of time pondering his resolutions, since he listed all of seventy resolutions to live by. (Franklin, by the way, listed only thirteen.) He made a note to remind himself "to read over these Resolutions once a week," just so that they would stay fresh on his mind. (Who could commit all seventy to memory, after all?) In his first resolution he vowed to live for the glory of God as his highest goal, and to devote himself to "the good and advantage" of all humanity—an admirable goal, to be sure, and one that framed his overall perspective on life.

We misunderstand Edwards if we neglect his serious resolve to sustain a constant focus on God as the purpose of his life in every detail. In January, 1723, when Edwards was nineteen years old, for instance, he resolved "that no other end but religion, shall have any influence at all on any of my actions; and that no action shall be, in the least circumstance, any otherwise than the religious end will carry it." This single-minded zeal for God was much more than an intellectual pursuit, though Edwards never separated study from piety. Just as he resolved to evaluate his spiritual life, he also vowed to nourish his intellectual curiosity, "to be continually endeavoring to find out some new invention and contrivance to promote" religion and morality. Most centrally these resolutions communicate the seriousness with which Edwards took life and his desire to "to live with all my might, while I do live."[10]

Spiders and Spirituality

This very discipline that drove Edwards's spiritual and moral convictions to live life with all the energy he had also inspired in him a deep fascination with nature. Many intellectuals in the eighteenth century shared this interest, including Franklin. While Franklin, however, dodged lightning bolts to comprehend electricity, Edwards took a very different approach: he observed spiders to learn about God.

Early in his ministry Edwards wrote and hoped to publish his experiments on "the wondrous and curious works of the spider." Edwards had ambitious plans for his "Spider Letter." He submitted it for publication with the *Philosophical Transactions* published by London's Royal Society, a prestigious scientific society headed by Sir Isaac Newton. Unfortunately, he was turned down—evidently someone had already published something compelling on spiders.[11] Even if Edwards's research on spiders did not break new scientific ground, science for its own sake was never his goal. True to Edwards's vow to devote all energies to God, even his research on spiders included a theological agenda. We may expect theologians to see God's handiwork in the beautiful scenes of nature—a brilliant sunset by the seashore, a marvelous starlit sky, or the perfect symmetry of birds in flight. But spiders? These most often provoke fear and disgust rather than admiration and divine inspiration! How many poems have been written in praise of the black widow? How many rhapsodies have waxed lovingly on the virtues of the brown recluse? Not many, if any. But this was precisely Edwards's point. When he searched the world, he found God's wonders in unexpected places. When he years later wrote his dissertation *Concerning the End for Which*

God Created the World, he described God's creation as a showplace for the glorious attributes of God. And he was most impressed by finding God's glorious attributes in even the most lowly and despised of creatures.

In his "Spider Letter," therefore, Edwards seized the chance to exalt "the wonders that are to be seen in the most despicable of animals." He was particularly impressed with the spiders' ability to fly without wings, and he loved to watch them "marching in the air from one tree to another," riding their webs. Even more fascinating was the sight of "vast multitudes of little shining webs and glistening strings, brightly reflecting the sun-beams, and some of them of a great length, and at such a height that one would think that they were tacked to the vault of the heavens"—in all "a very pleasing as well as surprising appearance." But he found "most astonishing" of all the apparent joy of the spiders in flight: "Very often there appears at the end of these webs, spiders sailing in the air . . . doubtless with abundance of pleasure" as they vaulted through the sky.

Yes, Edwards found great beauty and joy in the impressive work of the spider. And where Edwards found beauty and joy, he also found God. In his view, the spider displayed God's great "wisdom" in designing the spider's webbing—"that wonderful liquor with which their bottle tail is filled, that may so easily be drawn out so exceedingly fine," then quickly converted from a liquid to a material that is "so very rare as to be lighter than the air, and will so excellently serve to all their purposes." Moreover, Edwards contended, the spider displays God's "exuberant goodness," because God not only gave spiders what they needed to survive, God also saw to it that the spiders enjoyed their lives. In giving spiders the ability to weave webs and sail through the air, God showed concern "for the pleasure and recreation of all sorts of creatures, even the insects." Amazingly, in the spider, the lowest and most despised of such creatures, Edwards saw God's meticulous creativity and beauty of design. More importantly, however, he saw these detestable creatures as revealing the benevolence of a God who wants even the lowest of insects to experience joy.[12]

Divine Beauty and Truth in Nature and Scripture

If Edwards could find God's handiwork in spiders, he could find it almost anywhere. He never tired of pointing out the remarkable irony that even the most lowly beings communicated God's glory. But for all his love of nature, Edwards was far too much of a Calvinist to believe that we can learn as much about God by observing nature as we can by reading Scripture. In fact, without the Bible, we would not know how to recognize God's true influence in nature. In the eighteenth century this was monumentally important, because some prominent thinkers began to doubt Scripture's accuracy as a source of divine truth.

Granted, most intellectuals in Edwards's day believed in God and trusted the authority of Scripture to some extent. But even in this early stage of the modern period scholars began to use the latest research methods to examine the Bible, and a few thinkers concluded that the Bible contained contradictory and inaccurate historical information that cast doubt on its authority as a completely trustworthy, holy source of divine truth. Even the enlightened thinkers who did not attack Scripture began to stress that we can learn universal knowledge about God from nature without resorting to a particular group of ancient writings. As a result, intellectuals at the time compared the truth we can discover about God by observing the natural world

with the truth we can gain only from Scripture, and many put nature at least on a par with Scripture. Edwards opposed these claims. While he appreciated nature as a guide to godly truth, the most reliable knowledge was still found in Scripture. In Edwards's view, nature and the Bible should be read together; they were complementary, not contradictory.

Scripture and nature were intimately related, Edwards believed, but the relationship was not always clear. According to Edwards, while God speaks to us through both the natural world and the biblical texts, the "language" that God uses is something like a mysterious code that we need to decipher. The commonly accepted key to cracking the code to Scripture was an ancient method of reading called "typology." Beginning in the first century of the church, Christians believed that the Hebrew Bible (which Christians called the Old Testament) was intimately related to the Christian Scriptures (which Christians recognized as the New Testament). God spoke in both testaments, they believed, but the link between the two testaments was not always easy to understand. Some Old Testament texts seemed outdated or irrelevant in light of the New Testament. To solve this problem, Christians turned to typology to clarify the relation between the two testaments. We find examples of typology in Christian writers throughout history and even in the New Testament itself. In Romans 5:14, for instance, Paul refers to Adam as a "figure" or "type" from the Hebrew Bible that was fulfilled in Christ, the "new Adam." In this way, Christian writers found all kinds of types in the Old Testament that they believed symbolized God's fuller revelation in the New Testament.[13]

Typology fascinated Edwards. He spent hours scouring the Bible for types and then writing them down in his notebooks. In the first entry of one of these later notebooks, entitled "Types of the Messiah," he wrote that typology was a great method of teaching that was perfectly suited to human nature. Types in Scripture "enlighten and illustrate, and . . . convey instruction with impression, conviction and pleasure" while they also "help the memory." Further, Edwards maintained that biblical types are helpful because they conform to our "natural delight in the imitative arts, in painting, poetry, fables, metaphorical language [and] dramatic performances"—a tendency that "appears early in children." So, for Edwards, biblical types were not only useful in revealing the links between the Old and New Testaments; typological images were also poetic, instructive, and even entertaining communicators of God's glory.[14]

Nothing radical so far. Typology was an ancient, much relied-upon method of reading Scripture. But Edwards did not stop there. In an unconventional move, he used typology not only in unveiling divine messages in Scripture, but also in revealing God's presence in nature. He reasoned that since the God who inspired Scripture was the same God who created the world, nature and Scripture were intimately related. Both nature and Scripture revealed the beauty, excellency, and harmony of God.

As a twenty-five-year-old pastor in Northampton, Edwards pondered this natural-scriptural relationship in a notebook appropriately titled "Images of Divine Things" (previously titled "Shadows of Divine Things").[15] Early on in the notebook, Edwards wrote that "there is a great and remarkable analogy in God's works." In his reading of Scripture, together with his observation of nature, he was convinced that God used both means to communicate with us. Edwards asked rhetorically: "Why should we not suppose that [God] makes the inferior in imitation of the superior, the material of the spiritual, on purpose to have a resemblance and shadow of them?" Why not consider that

God created the entire physical world "as a shadow of the spiritual world"? This was an essential philosophical belief for Edwards. He strongly opposed materialistic explanations of the universe, such as that of English philosopher Thomas Hobbes, which taught that everything in the universe was material rather than spiritual, even God, if God existed at all. In opposition, Edwards embraced a typological view of the universe, in which the material world symbolized more essential spiritual realities. The material world, according to Edwards, was secondary to the spiritual universe.[16]

Edwards's notebooks are full of the wonderful analogies he found in nature that expressed much divine truth. These natural phenomena ran the full range from beautiful revelations of God to revolting images of Satan. For instance, he suggested that "the silkworm is a remarkable type of Christ" because, when the silkworm "dies, [it] yields us that of which we make such glorious clothing." Similarly, "Christ became a worm for our sakes, and his death finished that righteousness with which believers are clothed." On the darker side of nature, Edwards said, "ravens that with delight feed on carrion seem to be remarkable types of devils who with delight prey upon the souls of the dead. A dead, filthy, rotten carcass is a lively image of the soul of a wicked man that is spiritually and exceedingly filthy and abominable. . . . Such souls the devil delights in; they are his proper food." And in another example, Edwards even found a spiritual lesson in watching a game of cat and mouse. Observing that a cat's play "with a mouse that it has taken captive is a lively emblem of the way of the devil with many wicked" sinners, he reasoned that "a mouse is a foul, unclean creature, a fit type of a wicked" person. Furthermore, just as the cat plays with the doomed mouse, the

devil makes "sport with a wicked" sinner. As a cat lets a mouse think it is free while in reality the cat is in total control, so the devil fools sinners into thinking that they are free and properly religious while all the time the devil is in control until he finally devours them. In this way, by reading nature in biblical terms, Edwards deemed that "the Book of Scripture is the interpreter of the book of nature." Everything in nature has spiritual meaning; everything communicates something of the divine.[17]

The New Science and the Old Faith

The examples above are important for understanding Edwards, because they illustrate how this eighteenth-century minister and intellectual reconciled two powerful influences of his age—the Enlightenment's empirical, scientific emphasis on reason and the Reformed tradition's confessional, spiritual emphasis on biblical authority. In some ways our contemporary assumptions make it difficult to understand Edwards's interest in science. We look at Edwards through generations of conflicts between natural science and religion, punctuated by key moments like the 1925 Scopes "monkey" trial that positioned evolution versus the Bible in Dayton, Tennessee. As modern people we assume that natural science and theology are irreconcilable forms of thought. When we view Edwards from our post-Scopes perspective, we may be impressed that a Reformed theologian was so inclined toward scientific discovery. But Edwards was not unique in his day for being a minister-scientist. Ministers were intellectual leaders in the eighteenth century, and science was a common interest they had, alongside history, literature, and geography. A couple of generations after Edwards, natural science achieved a new status as the ultimate form of scientific research, separate from and, for many, superior to other forms of knowledge, including philosophy and theology. But in Edwards's world, most thinkers considered natural science and theology to be compatible ways of knowing about God's world. So in the eighteenth century it was not unusual to find ministers like Edwards investigating the natural world, while physicists like Isaac Newton studied apocalyptic Scriptures.[18]

Consider the example of Cotton Mather, a prominent minister in Boston. Mather represented the third generation of perhaps the most influential family of New England ministers. True to his intellectual heritage, Mather was a prolific writer on various subjects, from Reformed theology to natural science. (In fact, Mather was one of the few colonial ministers who wrote even more than Edwards!) Mather saw no conflict between natural science and Christian doctrine. Moreover, Mather saw no contradiction between the scientific exploration of nature and ideas that most modern people would consider superstitions. Intellectuals in Mather's generation read almanacs and considered astrology a valid scientific pursuit. They looked for signs of God's favor or judgment in the weather. And, as we all know, they took witchcraft very seriously, considering it a scientifically verifiable threat to religion and society.[19]

Mather played a pivotal role in the infamous witch trials in Salem, Massachusetts, in 1692. Chronologically, Edwards was not far removed from the witchcraft paranoia; accused witches were swinging from the gallows in Salem just eleven years before he was born. But much changed intellectually between the Salem witch trials and the beginning of Edwards's ministry. In his scientific observations, he studied nature fervently, but he never combined these scientific experiments with experiments to determine whether any of his parishioners were baking witch cakes or casting spells on one another. Though he worried a great deal about the spiritual influence of Satan in both church and society, he never accused anyone of being a witch or warlock, though his difficult church members may have tempted him to perform an exorcism! In just twenty years, therefore, the Salem witch trails had gone from being a serious legal and religious confrontation with Satan to a tragic embarrassment for New England ministers. For enlightened thinkers, the Salem witch trials were a prime illustration of the dangerous superstition of Reformed Christianity.

Thus, Edwards lived at the dawning of this transitional period, when intellectuals were beginning to see more conflicts than commonalities between traditional Christianity and natural explanations of the universe. The changes were

sometimes subtle and gradual. Most intellectuals in Edwards's day still believed God acted in the world, but in their view God acted through natural causes, not supernatural interventions. Isaac Newton, for instance, was a Christian with an intense interest in Scripture, but his revolutionary discoveries forced changes in traditional views of reality that in turn forced changes in traditional understandings of Christianity. Through the influence of Newton, eighteenth-century thinkers viewed the universe in mechanical terms. That is, everything in the universe is constantly in motion, regulated by gravity, and always moving in a perfectly synchronized pattern. In this view of reality there was little room for an interventionist God who violated natural laws at will and invaded the system with supernatural acts. For many enlightened thinkers, therefore, the new understanding of the universe called for a new view of divine intervention. God could no longer be actively involved in the details of daily life, continually intervening to control human actions and guide history through supernatural means. Instead, God became more distant, a creator who started the universe in motion and let it run on its own. At least this was the view of many intellectuals, who were often called deists, and their view of God directly clashed with the sovereign God that Edwards learned about from his childhood—and defended with all his intellectual powers.[20]

In response to this mechanistic view of the universe, Edwards argued for the spiritual and typological view of reality that we considered earlier. The beauty and harmony of the natural world were not just the result of natural laws that could work just fine without God. Instead, the harmony of the universe reflected the harmony of God. Natural laws were God's laws, and nothing occurred apart from the presence of God. In natural events, for instance, when an apple falls from a tree and gravity pulls it to the ground, God is involved. And in supernatural events, as when water turned to wine in a wedding at Cana, God was involved. Nothing happens apart from God because God upholds the universe in every moment of existence. In fact—and this is really profound—God actually *re-creates* the universe "out of nothing in every moment."[21] To the deists, then, who wanted to distance God from the universe, Edwards responded the opposite: God was intimately involved in every detail of the universe. (Not that God actually *approved* of everything that happened—more on that later, when we discuss the problem of evil.) For the philosophers among us, this was Edwards's version of "idealism," and it demonstrated that he was on the cutting edge of philosophical thought, though his version of philosophy proved rather than denied the sovereignty of God.

A New "Sense" of the Beauty of God

Edwards fully felt the sting of modern attacks on his faith. As he, too, had once questioned Reformed Christianity's apparent contradictions with the modern world, he knew how persuasive these challenges were. In his youth Edwards questioned how a just God could elect some to salvation while condemning others without regard to their own efforts. In regard to God's love, he once pondered how a loving God could condemn people to hell, even children.[22] Edwards even admitted that this idea of a sovereign God seemed "like a horrible doctrine to me."

But Edwards later experienced a radical transformation in his point of view on God's sovereignty. He grew to have "a *delightful* conviction" that God's sovereignty was "an exceeding pleasant, bright and sweet doctrine." That is, the

THE HILLS, SUN, MOON, STARS, CLOUDS, SKY...

idea of a God who elected some and damned others was transformed for Edwards from a "horrible" concept to a "sweet doctrine." Quite a change.

Edwards detailed this change in his *Personal Narrative*. Beginning when he was about seventeen, Edwards began to experience a new "inward, sweet delight in God and divine things"—a new perception of God that began as he read 1 Timothy 1:17 (KJV), "Now unto the King eternal, immortal, invisible, the only wise God, be honour and glory for ever and ever. Amen." Through his reading of this verse, Edwards felt "a sense of the glory of the divine being; a new sense, quite different from anything I ever experienced before." He then prayed over these words of Scripture, and his prayer was unlike any he had known; it was a prayer "with a new sort of affection." At this point, this young man who had been raised in a household filled with religious conversation and practice began to see familiar things in a new way. He now had "a new kind of apprehensions and ideas of Christ, and the work of redemption," which he described as "an inward, sweet sense" of God and salvation. At this point the teenage Edwards did what we would expect: he talked to his father, who counseled him in an affecting way. After talking with his father, he walked alone to a secluded place in a pasture. Here, Edwards "looked up on the sky and clouds" and then felt "a sweet sense of the glorious majesty and grace of God" that he could not clearly describe, though he expressed the new sense as "a sweet conjunction" between God's "majesty and meekness"—it was "a sweet and gentle, and holy majesty; and also a majestic meekness; an awful sweetness; a high, and great, and holy gentleness." But this was not a momentary vision that came and went as his earlier religious awakenings had. After this time, Edwards came to view everything differently. He now noticed "a calm, sweet cast, or appearance of divine glory, in almost everything." Again, Edwards especially saw God's beauty in nature as a significant element of his new experience: "God's excellency, his wisdom, his purity and love, seemed to appear in everything; in the sun, moon and stars; in the clouds, and blue sky; in the grass, flowers, trees; in the water, and all nature."

This sense of God's excellency was both spiritually engaging and philosophically profound. British philosophers and moralists wrote a lot about excellency as a universal sense of harmony and proportion. We are naturally attracted to harmony and repelled by disharmony and chaos. Edwards agreed, but he turned this philosophical study of harmony in spiritual directions. Excellency and harmony are beautiful to us because they reflect God's excellency, harmony, and beauty. God's excellency consists in the harmonious relations between the three persons of the Trinity, and this divine harmony is expressed in all creation. As Edwards thought about God's excellency, therefore, he was naturally entranced by nature: he spent hours observing the moon, sun, and stars. Above all, Edwards emphasized his new sense of beauty, his changed perspective. His key example was in his attitude toward thunderstorms. Before his new sense of God's glory, storms terrified him. But now his reaction to storms was the opposite: he celebrated them. He sensed God's power in the storms. As a storm approached, he studied it, watched "the lightnings play" and listened for "the majestic and awful voice of God's thunder: which often times was exceedingly entertaining, leading me to sweet contemplations of my great and glorious God."[23]

In these "sweet contemplations," Edwards thought much about heaven. To be sure, Edwards's reputation as a hellfire preacher would suffer dramatically if more people read his reflections on heaven. But for Edwards, heaven was primarily neither a self-serving and materialistic fantasy nor a relief from earthly hardships. Heaven's happiness

instead flowed from its eternal celebration of "divine love" and "holy communion with Christ." Heaven's great beauty was due to its holiness, which Edwards considered "the highest beauty" that put all other forms of beauty to shame. Holiness for Edwards was "of a sweet, pleasant, charming, serene, calm nature" that "brought an inexpressible purity, brightness, peacefulness and ravishment to the soul," making "the soul like a field or garden of God, with all manner of pleasant flowers" within it. Experiencing God's salvation truly, therefore, included a glimpse of the holiness of heaven and empowered a life marked with humble contemplation of God's ravishing beauty.

We find one of Edwards's best descriptions of a spiritually beautiful, heaven-centered life in a poem that he wrote about "a young lady" he knew in New Haven. The lady was Sarah Pierpont, and "young" was the proper description—she was thirteen when Edwards wrote the poem. In comparison, he was a ripe old age of twenty. He wrote this poem the same year he wrote the "Spider Letter." (Obviously he had more than arachnids on his mind!) The poem focused on the beauty Jonathan saw in Sarah Pierpont, but it was no romantic celebration of passionate love. Instead he praised the beauty of God that Pierpont communicated in her life. Edwards described Pierpont as one enthralled with God, delighted in God, caring only for divine things. She forgot about the world and looked forward to heaven, where she wanted "to be ravished with [God's] love, favor and delight, forever." Her thoughts and actions were godly, giving her "a strange sweetness in her mind," and constantly "full of joy and pleasure" that surprised all. She was calm, he wrote, had a "universal benevolence of mind," and liked "to wander in the fields and on the mountains," where she enjoyed the communion of God alone. Here we have an example of the religious person par excellence, the single-minded Christian, entranced with holy zeal that empowered a godly life. Edwards was obviously impressed; he and Pierpont married four years later.[24]

As these reflections on spiritual beauty indicate, to understand Edwards's theology, we must understand his religious experience. He would spend much of his career contemplating this new sense of divine things, which, for him, was something to celebrate and to study. He proclaimed it from the pulpit and spent hundreds of pages examining it rationally and biblically. In one of his early sermons, preached while he was a twenty-year-old pastor in Bolton, Connecticut, Edwards proclaimed that without the new sense of divine things we are spiritually blind. Without this new sense, we may know about God's truth, even be experts in Scripture, but we cannot truly "experience" God's beauty. He compared it to the difference between knowing that honey is sweet and actually tasting it. In a similar way, we can only truly experience God's

truth when we are regenerated and given a new sense to perceive the divine. Edwards expanded this view in one of his most famous sermons, "A Divine and Supernatural Light." Here we find Edwards the rational thinker, who could not allow the age of reason to extinguish the spiritual depth of his faith. Nothing was more reasonable, Edwards proclaimed, than the firm conviction that the mind cannot truly understand God on its own. When we are converted, God plants within us "a divine and supernatural light" that improves the reason, not by giving us new information about God—Scripture is sufficient for that—but by granting us a "true sense of the divine excellency" of God. It's not a matter of intellect, but of taste, a "sense of the heart." No wonder Jesus revealed his truth to uneducated disciples who could perceive the spiritual truth that the intellectual scribes and Pharisees missed. In an age of reason, therefore, Edwards proclaimed the truth perceivable only through the spirit and the heart, and he defended this claim on the ground of reason.[25]

But this new sense of divine things was not only an individual experience. It was significantly corporate. Edwards not only experienced it himself, he studied its power in the sermon and examined its effects in the revivals. This new experience of God was, in his view, the primary way God was acting in the world to bring about a new creation. Edwards continually cast his eyes on this new horizon, looking for God's activity in the world. This expectation fueled his preaching and shaped his interest both in ancient history and in current events, as he often scoured the news of the day, looking for "some news favorable to the interest of religion in the world."[26]

But if the ramifications of redemption were global, for Edwards nothing could be known without the local—his experiences of revival in New England churches. Here

Edwards grew from observer to practitioner. As a child he sat before his father's revival sermons, and these observations shaped his expectations for the possibilities of God's work. But his youthful observation of revival and his academic training empowered his own revival preaching, which began in earnest after he succeeded his grandfather, the great Solomon Stoddard, as pastor in Northampton, Massachusetts. Through his forty-seven-year ministry in Northampton, Stoddard had become a towering figure. Under his leadership the Northampton congregation grew to become the largest church outside of Boston in Massachusetts. Stoddard's legacy both rewarded and challenged Edwards throughout his ministry in Northampton. While Edwards would later suffer the consequences of disagreeing with his grandfather's polity on church membership and the sacraments, he fulfilled and surpassed Stoddard's

legacy as a great revival preacher. Stoddard had preached sporadic revival "harvests," but Edwards would contribute to a broader "Great Awakening" of revival fervor, and he devoted much of his theological enterprise to defending and articulating a revivalist vision.

CHAPTER TWO

An Affection for Revival

When many people think about Jonathan Edwards, they think about hell—and for good reason. His sermon "Sinners in the Hands of an Angry God" is the most read of his works, has been reprinted countless times in anthologies, and is, as historian Harry Stout notes, "arguably America's greatest sermon."[1] Why? It's certainly not because of the sermon's appealing subject matter. The sermon, after all, fixates on the threat of hell for all people, here and now—hardly a cheery topic. Even Edwards would admit that the subject of the sermon is terrifying. "Sinners" makes historians

cringe for another reason: while it is Edwards's most popular work, it does not come close to representing his
thought, especially the poetic beauty and grace in his theology. Nevertheless "Sinners" is considered a great sermon
for at least two reasons. First, it represents one of the most
important events in colonial America—the outburst of religious revivals often called the "Great Awakening" that
reached its zenith in New England in 1740–42. Second,
despite its detestable subject matter, "Sinners" is a master-
piece of rhetorical effectiveness and vivid imagery. After
reading it, who could forget such lines as:

> The God that holds you over the pit of Hell, much as
> one holds a spider, or some loathsome insect over the
> fire, abhors you, and is dreadfully provoked: his wrath
> towards you burns like fire; he looks upon you as
> worthy of nothing else, but to be cast into the fire; he
> is of purer eyes than to bear to have you in his sight;
> you are ten thousand times more abominable in his
> eyes, than the most hateful venomous serpent is in
> ours. . . . 'tis nothing but his hand that holds you
> from falling into the fire every moment.[2]

Can you feel the heat? Edwards hoped so, and not
because he was sadistic or even pessimistic; he was not. And
it's not that he worried that his audience needed to be convinced that hell was real. Unlike today, few eighteenth-
century people doubted that hell existed. As Edwards saw
it, the people's problem wasn't belief, but conviction.
Edwards worried that his hearers were aware that hell
existed, but they were "not sensible of this"; they did not
believe that the threat of hell, being doomed to eternal
punishment, applied to them.[3] Edwards exposed this false
sense of security with his personal, sensible images. He
wanted his hearers to "feel" hell, to experience its threat in

the sermon because the lack of sensibility to hell was a serious impediment to salvation. The committed and passionate pastor, therefore, addressed his congregation personally with sensible images of terror not to condemn them, but to prevent them from eternal condemnation. Like all revivalists, Edwards aimed to awaken sinners from their drowsy spiritual state. In the revivals, Edwards hoped that sinners would not only comprehend theological ideas but have an experience of the gospel that would change their lives, before it was too late.

The Psychology of Revival

In spite of the wide recognition of his "Sinners" sermon, Edwards was not the only famous preacher in the eighteenth century, nor was he the most impressive. (That honor goes to George Whitefield.) But Edwards was the superior theologian of the revivals. More than anyone else, Edwards studied the revivals intensely, rightly making his

knowledge of them renowned in international circles. He sought to know the "awakenings" inside out—from the psychology of religious experience generated by revivals to their social effects and implications for churches and communities. Four years before he preached "Sinners," Edwards's expertise in revival was already secured by his *Faithful Narrative of the Surprising Work of God* (1737), which, translated and published in several European countries, became a classic description of revival.[4] In fact, John Wesley, the British founder of Methodism, admired it so much that he published his own edition of the work; as a result, Edwards's views on revival influenced the Wesleyan movement.[5]

What made the *Faithful Narrative* so influential? The *Faithful Narrative* described in detail the revival ignited by Edwards's preaching in Northampton in the 1730s. Edwards was an acute observer of God's active work in his community, and found the revivals surprising in many ways. But his description in the *Faithful Narrative* was also an argument: Edwards championed the value of revivals against claims that the revivals were no more than excessive religious rants fueled by wild enthusiasm, strange new revelations, and emotionally charged worship services that made a mockery of respectable worship and orthodox doctrine. Against these accusations, Edwards's *Narrative* was a calming influence—no such religious delirium was taking over Northampton. The revivals were uncommon, but they were also accompanied by sound doctrine and good moral results.

While Edwards sought to calm those who were nervous about revivalist excesses, he also hoped to excite those in America and Europe who craved a worldwide revival that would convert the masses. And hopefully, he thought, this move of God was starting in the Northampton awaken-

ings. These revivals were surprising, because religious concern had decreased in the community. Before the revivals young people neglected religion and were "addicted to night-walking," often "frequenting the tavern," participating in "lewd practices," and staying out far too late at night "in conventions of both sexes, for mirth and jollity, which they called frolics." Theological challenges also inhibited revival. The people of Northampton were greatly concerned about a theological movement called Arminianism, which deemphasized the sovereign operations of God in conversion and emphasized human free will, encouraging people to take charge of their own salvation.

Remarkably, the religious climate began to change, however, and people became more preoccupied with religious concerns, sometimes so much that they began neglecting their secular occupations. Edwards attributed the change to several influences—certainly his preaching on justification by faith had something to do with it. These sermons cut though the Arminian thicket to call people back to the basic idea that fueled the Reformation of Martin Luther and John Calvin—that God graciously justifies people through faith alone, not through any effort of their own. In addition, two unexpected deaths directed the attention of young people toward religion—a young man died quickly after "being violently seized with a pleurisy," and a young woman became a model of piety from her deathbed, "warning and counseling" others about the need for salvation.

Regardless of the contributing factors, however, the move was under way—many people in Edwards's community turned from worldly interest to spiritual zeal, set their eyes on heaven and worried about "dropping into hell" at any moment, and even "the vainest and loosest" of sinners experienced "great awakenings." The statistics were impressive: over three hundred people converted in six months, and about as many men were converted as women, unusual, since most of the time women outnumbered men in colonial churches. And the revivals were universal in other ways. They attracted not only the young, which was expected, but even the old, which was rare; it was almost unheard of "that any were converted past middle age." The revivals were even racially diverse. Edwards observed that many African Americans were converted during the contagious awakenings, which spread throughout the villages far more quickly than usual.[6]

But in his *Faithful Narrative* Edwards was not content to provide an overview of the revivals, quoting numbers of converted and estimating the many influences on communities. He also investigated the psychology of redemption, clarifying how awakenings occurred in individuals. Ever the observer, Edwards took a scientific interest in examining the effects of revival on the mind. What he found surprised him. While he had been trained by his father in the Puritan tradition to believe that salvation followed a particular order, a process of stages toward redemption that could be identified, he discovered that people did not always experience conversion in the expected stages. He found instead that nearly every conversion experience was unique. Two examples were especially important.

The first was Abigail Hutchinson, a woman who grew ill and died but experienced true conversion before her death. From a sensible family, not at all prone to "enthusiasm" in religion, she was a quiet, reserved person. Like most who were converted, she experienced real terror; she was awakened to a sense of her own evil, the sin that separated her from God. But in time she experienced a breakthrough, a new "sense of the glory of God's truth," and a relish for the "sweetness" of divine things. After this, she did not dread her impending death, but, to the contrary, she actually

looked forward to it. As one might expect after reading "Sinners," Edwards's description of her yearning for death is graphically morbid. He reports that on one occasion her brother read aloud to her some of the most unedifying of biblical passages, including the descriptions of worms eating a corpse found in Job. Disgusting? Perhaps. But not for Abigail Hutchinson. She smiled at the description, and "said it was sweet to her to think of her being in such circumstances." Morbid aspirations aside, she died quite peacefully, "as a person that went to sleep, without struggling."

Edwards's second example was four-year-old Phoebe Bartlett. His description of little Phoebe is enough to make modern parents recoil. Phoebe was fascinated by religion and was constantly afraid that she would go to hell. Her fears of eternal torment devastated her, and she adjourned to her closet five or six times daily to pray for deliverance. Finally, one day she experienced God's presence, and her parents immediately recognized a transformation in her speech and composure. From this point Phoebe's major concern was for her friends who were not yet converted, and she witnessed to them constantly. Edwards's description of this little girl revealed much about the breadth of the awakenings, demonstrating that anyone could be converted to a true knowledge of God and a mature faith— even a four-year old. Even more, however, the Phoebe Bartlett story reveals to us today the distance between our time and Edwards's. While most of us in the modern world would be disturbed at the thought of a child obsessing over hell, Edwards considered it constructive, a healthy spiritual exercise. Hell, after all, was a real threat, even for children, especially since children were more likely to die before reaching maturity in Edwards's day than in ours. Given the constant threat of death, anxiety over hell led to pursuit of salvation, which was a child's only eternal hope.

As Edwards's description of morbid fantasies of worm-eaten corpses and a child obsessed with hell aptly demonstrates, the revivals were nothing if not surprising. While Edwards worked hard to understand the phenomena, in the end he found them to be as mysterious as the God who inspired them. In the next century, beginning with the great preacher Charles Finney, revival became more predictable, more of a science. Preachers honed their skills at producing revivals, relied on certain tried and true methods, and revivals resulted. This legacy that began with Finney and reached new heights with modern evangelists like Billy Graham was unheard of in Edwards's time. While Edwards and his contemporaries used methods to publicize and stimulate revivals, including publications like Edwards's *Faithful Narrative*, they also believed that revivals originated with God, not human effort. Revivals were mysteries, therefore, and their mysteriousness fed the controversy surrounding them.

In particular, the 1730s revival in Northampton and surrounding areas ended abruptly and ominously. Like most people of this time, Edwards believed in a real Satan who abided with people always, watching their every move while devising ways to hijack the gospel and to elude God's plans. Edwards was surprised that Satan seemed strangely quiet during the revival, but this satanic silence ended with tragedy. At the height of revival, a man of Northampton attempted suicide. Though his attempt was unsuccessful and the man subsequently repented of his sin, this happy ending was short-lived. The revival ebbed and Satan made his evil presence known once again when another man in town attempted suicide by slicing his throat; he succeeded. Most alarmingly, as Edwards wrote, this man "was a gentleman of more than common understanding, of strict morals, religious in his behavior, and a useful honorable

person in the town"—and he was Edwards's uncle. When Satan drove this respectable and religious man to suicide, the community was stunned. Even worse, others in the town began to contemplate suicide. Even pious persons who were never prone to depression felt the urge to end their lives, "as if somebody had spoke to 'em, 'Cut your own throat, now is a good opportunity; now, NOW!' So that they were obliged to fight with all their might to resist it." The revivals were abruptly over; Satan's influence had returned in full force.[7]

The Great Awakening: Godly Deliverance or Satanic Scheme?

After the events of Northampton, many believed that Satan not only besieged the revivals but created them. As such, the revivals that Edwards praised as the gracious blessing of God were, in the view of some, actually a scheme of hell. The renewed outburst of revivals in the early 1740s, the "Great Awakening," ignited controversy. For those who supported revivals, the Great Awakening was an answer to pious dreams. For its opponents, revivals were the epitome of satanic encroachment on Christian territories.

Depending on the perspective, therefore, the promise or the problem of revival reached a crescendo with the preaching of George Whitefield, a British companion of Methodist founders John and Charles Wesley. Whitefield virtually invented the vocation of the traveling evangelist. Often called "the Grand Itinerant," he preached the message of the "new birth" to more people than ever before, sailing to America seven times, most often in preaching tours that extended through the colonies. Though he was an Anglican, his preaching crossed denominational boundaries. He preached in churches and outside churches, befriending ministers of numerous traditions while challenging and alienating others with his extemporaneous, dramatic sermons.[8] Whitefield's tour through New England intensified revival activity and criticism on various fronts. While Whitefield was divisive in his own preaching, his controversial effect on the colonies was tame compared to that of preachers who followed him in itinerant evangelism. James Davenport was the most extreme example. Though he was well educated and evidently had some gifts for ministry, Davenport personified what doubters of revival feared most—an unstable preacher who divided communities and pitted congregations against their clergy. Davenport preached aggressive sermons, attacked several prominent ministers as unconverted false teachers, and generally wreaked havoc in various communities. Eventually he was arrested for disturbing the peace and banished from Connecticut, but much damage had been done to the

reputation of revivals.[9] Edwards was as horrified by Davenport's unruly preaching as anyone. Davenport was a menace and needed to be stopped, Edwards believed, and he led a committee of ministers that disciplined Davenport and convinced him to recant. But much of the damage to the revival cause had been done.

Much to Edwards's disappointment, therefore, the revivals, which had so much promise for heavenly harmony, often provoked chaos. Congregationalists divided between "new light" defenders of revival and "old light" opponents, with little room for navigation between these two sides. And yet that is precisely what Edwards tried to do from the pulpit and in print. In 1741, soon after Davenport had disturbed many with his wild preaching, Edwards was invited to preach a sermon at Yale College entitled "The Distinguishing Marks of a Work of the Spirit of God," which attempted to separate the good from the bad in the revivals.[10] Five years later Edwards published a more complete examination of the revivals in his *Treatise Concerning Religious Affections.*

In the midst of the controversy, Edwards knew how difficult it was to find a place to stand outside the commotion. Given that revival was related to the most vital of all concerns—salvation—and given that the participants in the debates were sharply divided, Edwards knew that the most difficult problem was evaluating revival accurately and impartially. The "dust and smoke" of divisive debate, Edwards said, made it "difficult to write impartially," yet he knew that an impartial evaluation of revival was vital to the spiritual welfare of the local churches and perhaps the colony or even the continent. Edwards also knew that as difficult as it was to write impartially, it was even harder to read impartially, though he urged his readers to try. Edwards cautioned that both sides of the debate would want to reject some of his ideas. Many who supported revival would find much of their cherished views put down, and many who opposed revival would be outraged by Edwards's support of what they considered to be insults to decorum and respectability in religion. Edwards knew he would not please all, but he hoped to inform all about the most important questions in life, including "What is the nature of true religion?" Certainly no question was more vital, and yet, in Edwards's view, no question was more debated and confused. The revivals sparked the debate and the confusion, but the central issue was the nature of true religion itself: what is true religious experience, and how do we know that our religious experience is valid?[11]

Introducing the Religious Affections

One of the greatest expressions of Jonathan Edwards's theology surrounds what he termed the "religious affections"; he argued that without understanding them we cannot understand religious experience. Unaware of the religious affections and how they operate, we are clueless about how God relates to us, and we have no way of knowing whether our religious experiences are the holy effects of God or the counterfeit deceits of Satan. How, then, should we understand the affections? First, we should not confuse affections with "passions." Edwards claimed that opponents of the revivals fell into this trap: viewing the revivals as unruly, chaotic, and passionate religion run wild, with no thought to decorum or proper doctrine and no room for the intellect at all. Edwards wanted nothing to do with this kind of revival. He opposed any simplistic separation of "head" from "heart" in religion. True religion, Edwards believed, united the head and the heart—both were needed to understand and worship God properly.

The affections, therefore, are not unruly and anti-intellectual passions. In fact, Edwards called them "affections of the mind," and he worked to demonstrate how the affections and the mind worked together. He did so by first pointing out that we relate to the world with the "understanding," which is our intellectual ability, our capability to observe and reflect. Through our understanding we can recognize the difference between a circle and a triangle, know that $1+3=4$, and even calculate the acceleration of gravity. But we are more than our intellects, impressive as they are. We are not mere logical machines, objective observers and evaluators of everything we encounter. Some things and people attract us, while others repel us. To explain this reality, Edwards said that, aside from the understanding, we all have a power called the "inclination," and this is our ability to be "inclined" one way or another in response to all that we understand. Let's use our

sense of taste to illustrate the point. While in line at the local cafeteria, I encounter both broccoli and brownies. Not only can I easily taste and smell both foods, if I wanted, I could even study the texture and chemical makeup of both so that I could gain a full knowledge of both broccoli and brownies. But when it comes to eating one or the other, I am more inclined toward brownies than broccoli. All inclinations are different. Believe it or not, some people would much prefer to eat broccoli than to eat brownies! But all must be inclined one way or another to some extent.

Edwards noted that most people used terms other than "inclination" to refer to the same ability. We sometimes refer to the inclinations as the "heart"—when I think of broccoli and brownies, my heartfelt preference is for the brownies. And when we do something to act on our inclination, we call that action the "will." When I reach past the broccoli dish and pick up a brownie, I have acted on my inclination, showing that I am willing to eat the brownie. Of course there are various degrees of inclination. Given the choice between broccoli and brownies, I'm strongly inclined toward the brownies. But if the choice is between brownies and ice cream (and I can't have both), I'm more slightly inclined toward the brownies. In some cases inclinations are weak, in other cases they are strong. Edwards called strong inclinations the "affections." More specifically, the affections are the "more vigorous and sensible exercises" of the inclinations. The affections move beyond cold calculation to fervent inclination. Affections stir us up, excite us, and move us forward. Affections are intellectual—we have to know something before it can affect us—but when it affects us, it involves not only our minds but our hearts and bodies as well.

Edwards's crucial point is that when we talk about true

religion, we are talking about affections. True religion is never "weak, dull and lifeless" but instead involves "fervent exercises of the heart." Can you imagine Paul telling the church at Rome to accept a lifeless religion? Never. Instead, he charged them to "be . . . fervent in spirit" (Rom. 12:11). After all, God is the greatest power in the universe, and who could believe that the appropriate response to God's salvation is lukewarm and lifeless faith? Surely not. As Edwards passionately conveyed, the only appropriate response to God was hearty praise and zeal, the stuff of religious affections.[12]

While preaching the power and fervency of religious affections he was constantly on guard against those who confused affections with anti-intellectual passions coupled with wild, unorthodox theologies. The affections, Edwards argued, should be tied closely to the mind and controlled by the Holy Spirit. While passions overtake the mind and run amok, true religious affections are grounded in the intellect and God's abiding presence. Edwards said, "There must be light in the understanding, as well as an affected fervent heart, where there is heat without light, there can be nothing divine or heavenly in that heart," so Davenport and other radical enthusiasts beware. And yet "light without heat, a head stored with notions and speculations, with a cold and unaffected heart" is also useless, because if divine truths are "rightly understood, they will affect the heart."[13]

But things are not always what they seem. How do we know that our religious experience is genuine, that our affections are holy? Most affections, after all, are not religious. Affection for money drives greed, for instance, and affection for glory drives ambition. Affections are the root of most activity, both good and bad, secular and religious. Christians in Edwards's time were keenly interested in the

51

question of assurance; they wanted to know that they were among the elect, saved by God from eternal damnation. They wanted to know that their religious experiences were genuine—that they were experiencing the operations of God's spirit in their lives and not being deceived by Satan's nefarious influences. The revivals intensified this desire to know whether religious experience was true or false. Were the revivals godly, or satanic? Were those who experienced revival conversions part of a widespread movement of God or a diabolical, satanic scheme intended to destroy Christianity? Edwards cautioned against putting the issue in such extreme terms, judging all revivals as good or bad. The revivals were godly at heart, but God's plans were always Satan's targets, and the revivals were no exception. How, then, were Christians to know if their religious affections were genuine?

Always the analyst, Edwards advised Christians to examine the evidence, and he provided two lists of "signs" that people could use to judge their religious affections. Edwards first listed "negative signs," or signs that *do not* help us to judge whether religious affections are true or false. This list surprised many, Edwards realized, because it included signs that many people commonly assumed were good indicators of righteousness. For example, many assumed that zealous affections for divine things were always motivated by the Holy Spirit. Many were enthused by revival, and this excitement drove them to extravagant, sometimes bizarre behaviors, including loud praise and excited body movements. To supporters of revival who relied upon this high excitement to prove the validity of affections, Edwards cautioned that excited affections are not necessarily genuine. Take the story of the children of Israel as told in Exodus, for example. After the miraculous crossing of the Red Sea, they praised God with high affections, excited to be God's people in the wilderness. But in time these affections cooled, and the children of Israel busied themselves carving an idolatrous golden calf to worship. And yet Edwards also cautioned those who dismissed all revivals precisely because of the extravagant affections and body movements they often included. Edwards argued that all affections of the mind will have some effect on the body. Some affections are holy, some are unholy, but all affections move us, involving all of who we are, including our bodies. In the final analysis, then, mere excited affections and bodily gyrations proved nothing. Either God or Satan could incite them.[14]

Edwards dismissed other common signs as well, including the idea that genuine faith can be proved in Christians because they talk a lot about religion, quote the Bible incessantly, and seem to go through all the stages of conversion. Beware these signs! They may be indicators of true affections, but they may not. Imagine the frustration of Edwards's readers. With his list of negative signs, he had devastated many of their most cherished ideas about what conversion looked like.

However, Edwards also directed his readers to "positive signs," which provided reliable evidence that affections were holy.[15] But first Edwards cautioned his readers against using these signs to evaluate the spiritual lives of others; trying to judge one's friends and neighbors to determine which are true Christians and which are hypocrites may have been an entertaining pastime in the eighteenth century (and may still be!), but Edwards wanted nothing to do with it. He believed that the Bible gave solid guidance that helps us to come to approximate judgments about others so that we can avoid being led astray by false teachers; however, God never gave us the ability to see into another person's soul and know that person's salvation with certainty. That's God's prerogative. So Edwards offered his list of "signs of truly gracious and holy affections" to assist his

readers in judging their own religious experiences, not as a license to police the spiritual lives of the community.

Edwards led off his list with the basics: truly holy affections come from God; they are "spiritual, supernatural and divine"—not from our own imaginations. The truly converted have the Holy Spirit within them, empowering their affections as a "supernatural spring of life and action." To explain, Edwards compared the Spirit's work to light. Those who are converted do not just see the Spirit's light, and it does not just shine on them as the sun shines on the earth. Instead, the Spirit communicates itself to the converted so that they shine from within. He called this indwelling of the Spirit "a new inward perception," a "spiritual sense" that enlightens the mind so that it is sensitive to the divine. It's not that the converted have a new sixth sense that allows them to see visions that the unconverted do not; the new spiritual sense does not reveal extravagant visions or new worlds. Visions may be revealed by God or Satan, and even when a vision comes from God it does not necessarily indicate that the person who sees the vision is godly—as greedy Balaam's conversation with his pestering donkey proves. The new spiritual sense, therefore, is not a new intellectual capacity that enables us to receive new revelations. Instead, the Spirit enlightens the mind so that we can understand God better and recognize divine beauty in the world like never before. Edwards illustrated this point with the sense of taste—knowing that honey is sweet is not the same as tasting the honey and experiencing the sweetness. Likewise, before conversion we may know that God is holy and beautiful, but after conversion we experience the holiness and beauty of God firsthand. Gracious affections, therefore, are not anti-intellectual passions; they actually *improve the mind*, enhancing our senses so that we can understand God's truth, beauty, and movements in ways that the unconverted cannot.[16]

While Edwards's signs called for serious introspection and examination of the psyche, his final and most important sign was much more externally visible. "Gracious and holy affections," he said, "have their exercise and fruit in Christian practice." Specifically, if we are empowered by holy affections, we will behave like good Christians; we will be moral, faithful in worship and service to others, and humble. And this Christian activity will not be something we do in just our spare time. Instead, Christian work will be our major concern throughout our lives until we die. Edwards's critical point is that conversion is not just an inward change, an individual experience fueled by introspection and contemplation. Instead, if our affections are truly holy, they will move us to action. "Grace," he wrote, "is not an unactive thing; there is nothing in heaven or earth of a more active nature" than God's redeeming activity. The godly heart is always connected to godly practice as cause and effect, as surely as the sun is the source of light and a fountain is the source of a stream. If we are looking for evidence that our affections are holy and our faith is sincere, we should first look at what we do. "Christian practice," said Edwards "is the principal sign by which Christians are to judge, both of their own and others' sincerity of Godliness"—no amount of intensive introspection can replace the assurance gleaned from a godly life. Jesus said as much with his illustration "Ye shall know them by their fruits" (Matt. 7:16). Jesus did not say that we can judge a tree by its leaves or flowers, Edwards observed. Likewise, we should not judge people "by their talk," including "the good story they tell of their experiences," or by their outward displays of religious feeling and testimonies of devotion. In evaluating the sincerity of religious experience, actions are ultimately more reliable than words. "Hypocrites may much more easily be brought to talk like saints, than to act like saints."[17]

By closing his list of signs with religious practice, Edwards played his trump card against those who attacked the revivals for their overly heated passions and erratic behaviors. The chief of these critics was prominent Boston minister Charles Chauncy, whose *Seasonable Thoughts on the State of Religion in New England* had condemned the revivals to an international readership, blasting revivals for doing little more than stirring up anti-intellectual passions that corrupted true religion rather than supporting it. Edwards felt the sting of this criticism because, as the James Davenport case had proved, it was often valid. So in the last sign of *Religious Affections*, published after the

revivals had subsided, Edwards responded that godly practice, not enthusiastic behavior, was the chief sign of true religious experience. The final test of revival's validity was whether or not it produced faithful Christians.

In the revivals known as the Great Awakening, therefore, Edwards was one of revival's most avid observers. While preaching for revival, Edwards also investigated the revivals as thoroughly as he could. He examined the awakenings for their impact on churches and communities. But more fervently he studied how the revivals affected individual believers. He searched for clues into how the awakenings worked in the soul to move people from spiritual deadness to an embrace of the gospel. For Edwards the revivals were more than curious spectacle—though they were certainly that. More importantly, the revivals revealed key insights into how the mind worked and how God worked with the mind in all its intellectual and spiritual capacities.

Though Edwards was the best "scientist" of revival phenomena, he was far from an objective observer. He yearned for revival, preached revivalist sermons, and collaborated with others who shared his view that the awakenings were the best hope for promoting true religion. For Edwards, revivals were vital not only for his day but for all of history. In 1739 he preached a long series of sermons later titled *A History of the Work of Redemption*. Here, Edwards unveiled history as a tapestry of God's design for the world's redemption, a history that involved not only earthly history, but the history of the entire cosmos, including heaven and hell. In this grand view, revival played a central role in history's progress. Like most other Protestants, Edwards was on the lookout for the millennium, the time of Christ's thousand-year reign over the earth, and he watched for signs in world history and local events, all read through the lens of Scripture. Among the greatest signs both locally and internationally was revival success. Surely, Edwards thought, revivals were a main strategy in God's plan to redeem the world. Edwards cherished his own place in this plan, and he hoped that his preaching and writing in support of revival would contribute to a divine purpose of cosmic proportions. As we have seen, revival controversies forced Edwards to temper his optimism. Though the hope surged within him, he recognized that he was part of a spiritual war that pitted good versus evil. And as with any war there would be setbacks and casualties. In the next chapter we will consider how Edwards himself became a casualty in the spiritual warfare that he saw raging all around him.

CHAPTER THREE

Exodus from Northampton

By 1750, Jonathan Edwards was a well-known preacher and authority on revivalism. While George Whitefield was the most famous preacher of the eighteenth century, Edwards's notoriety was not far behind. As revivals stirred excitement and controversy from the American colonies to Europe, Edwards earned a reputation as a leading expert. While he did not crave celebrity as an end in itself, Edwards relished the central role he played in promoting revival throughout Christendom. And though this international reputation was important to Edwards, his ministry in Northampton was his primary concern. It was here, in this Massachusetts town, that Edwards did most of his preaching, and, as a result, Northampton gained a reputation as a model of revival success. Nevertheless, Edwards's happy days in Northampton came to a premature and abrupt end;

the escalation of revivals that he had worked and prayed for came crashing down. By the time he published *Religious Affections* in 1746, the revivals were mere memories, and they were replaced by strife and division. And by 1750, despite his international fame, Edwards was dismissed from his pastorate, rejected decisively by a church he had served for two decades. A council of ministers from ten churches in the area voted for Edwards's dismissal, and when the male church members voted, they overwhelmingly rejected Edwards by a final tally of 230 to 23.[1]

Why this dramatic reversal of fortunes? His humiliating exit likely resulted from a combination of factors, including deep-seated theological convictions as well as trivial disputes and personality conflicts. But two controversies were particularly damaging to Edwards's reputation in Northampton. The first was a case of youthful rebellion that degenerated into a crisis of sexual ridicule that embarrassed several prominent families. The second was a painful struggle that pitted Edwards against his grandfather Stoddard's legacy. In the end, Edwards lost. Despite his international reputation as a renowned revivalist and theologian, Edwards's authority at home could not overcome the backlash that resulted when he abandoned his grandfather's revered church practice.

Discovering the "Young Folks' Bible"

The drama that was to become one of Edwards's most divisive struggles in Northampton was set off by, of all things, a collection of illustrated medical manuals. Young men in the church were, Edwards discovered, amusing themselves with drawings focusing on the female anatomy. Ringleaders Timothy Root, his cousin Simeon, and Oliver Warner, all in their twenties, were using midwifery books as an

eighteenth-century version of pornography, which was in itself bad enough from Edwards's viewpoint. But in actions even more troubling, they used the information in these books to harass young women, arrogantly and insensitively, telling crude jokes about their menstrual cycles and other private matters.[2] As the overseer of the moral life of the church, a prominent and powerful guardian of virtue in the community, Edwards was disgusted by these behaviors. Moreover, by this time Edwards himself had daughters at home. This kind of sexual taunting must have personally angered him. These men were members of his church, and we can be certain that Edwards must have been deeply disappointed. Just a few years earlier he had praised the young people for their affecting response to revivals; now the situation with the youth had reversed, turning his praise into anger and profound embarrassment.

Though this behavior of these young men was clearly scandalous, the way Edwards chose to deal with them ignited outrage among many prominent citizens in the community. And the fallout proved to be the beginning of the end for Edwards's tenure in Northampton. The fateful process began when Edwards collected evidence of the offenses and brought it to the church for public consideration. After addressing the violations in a sermon, Edwards called church members to serve on a special committee to investigate the accused. With the help of the committee, Edwards hoped to resolve the crisis and discipline the offenders appropriately. But at this point the crisis escalated. When he called for a meeting of the committee at his house, Edwards revealed to the entire congregation all the names of the people who were to report—without distinguishing the accused from innocent witnesses. Some of those whose names were called took offense at Edwards's lack of discretion. And, most unfortunately for Edwards, some of those who were offended were from leading families in the community. In addition, many believed that Edwards made a public issue out of a matter that could and should have been dealt with privately. In Edwards's view, the offense was public, and so should be the discipline; but as the case progressed, Edwards's authority in the community suffered.

In Edwards's view this case was clearly symptomatic of spiritual problems that ran deeper than young lust and taunting, as serious as these issues were. Not only were the offenders behaving scandalously, they flaunted their disrespect for authority. In a biblical culture where scriptural authority was paramount, Timothy Root joked that the midwife manual was "the young folks' Bible." Moreover, throughout the committee's deliberation on the matter, the accused men disrespected Edwards and those he had called together to investigate. As the committee met, Timothy and Simeon Root left without permission to go to the tavern for a drink. Upon their return, the eloquent and insubordinate Timothy boldly pronounced that he didn't

"care a fart" or a "turd" for the committee. Just to prove they were serious in their rebellion, the men—remember, they were all in their twenties—went out for a game of leapfrog in Edwards's backyard. But in the end, the committee's punishments were virtual slaps on the wrist; Root and the other main offenders had only to confess their violations of church authority without ever owning up to the embarrassing sexual violations. Edwards, on the other hand, would pay a much heavier price later. But we will discuss that more in a bit.[3]

For now, it is important to understand that both this scandalous behavior and its relative tolerance made it painfully clear to Edwards that the revivals that once lifted the spiritual condition of Northampton were gone. Just as the young people had led the way in responding to revival's upswing, so now they themselves indicated the departure of spiritual blessings. And Edwards could not be nonchalant about revival's fading influence. In his view, the Christian world was embroiled in a spiritual war that was just as real as the military conflicts that constantly loomed between England and France. Revival success was essential to that spiritual combat between Christ and Satan, and as a soldier in God's cause it was his duty to work on behalf of the gospel to every possible extent. So while some viewed the "young folks' Bible" case as a repugnant yet minor case of youthful crudeness, Edwards was utterly convinced that it was a sure sign of Satan's encroachment in his community.

Battling the Stoddard Legacy: The Communion Controversy

The "young folks' Bible" case was just the beginning of the troubles between Edwards and his church, as a far more serious crisis loomed. But this time the dispute was more substantial, involving cherished convictions about the nature of the church. And this issue that finally ruptured the relationship between Edwards and Northampton was not new. It was an old argument that was particularly characteristic of the Puritan tradition.

Soon after arriving in New England in the previous century, Puritans constructed "Bible commonwealths," regionally based societies for government in which the church was central. And in order for the church to gain such a powerful voice as to speak for the town as a whole, the church could not be a small gathering of saints separated from the rest of society. Church and town needed to be united. Yet, at the same time, Puritans craved "purity" in the church. So while it needed to be a powerful force in the world, the church could not seize its power by sacrificing obedience to the gospel. Puritans, then, sought a balance. The church needed to be as pure as possible (or composed of members who were authentic Christians), but it could not stress purity to the extent that only a pious few met the standards of membership. The question was how to achieve the proper balance between purity and power in the church. What should the qualifications be for joining the church in full membership and receiving the sacraments?[4]

At no point in their history were Puritans able to develop a single answer to this question that pleased everyone. However, a majority view had developed early on in the Massachusetts Bay Colony. According to the Massachusetts Bay position, full membership in the church required that candidates not only be moral in life and orthodox in doctrine, but they also had to provide evidence that they had experienced a true, life-altering conversion. This evidence—usually in the form of a testimony to the experience—had to be presented to the church and judged valid before candidates could be admitted to full membership. Generally accepted though it was, this policy

produced problems. As the century progressed, fewer and fewer candidates presented themselves for full membership. Perhaps the expectations were too high? And since only full members could present their children for baptism, fewer and fewer children were coming under the care of the churches. For the church's power and survival, something needed to be done.

The solution came in the Half Way Covenant of 1662, a strategy worked out by a special synod of ministers. In particular, the Half Way Covenant sought to address the issue posed by the large number of adults who had been baptized in the church, grown up under its care, but never testified to a converting faith and, therefore, never become full members. These "half way" members did not, in accord with the Massachusetts Bay position, have the privilege of full membership, including the very important ability to present their children for baptism. Quite simply, the 1662 decision reversed this by allowing "half way" members to have their children baptized in the church. The church, therefore, could maintain its emphasis on purity (these halfway members were still not full members with the rights to voting on church decisions and taking Communion) and still make strides to secure its influence over the next generation.[5] Problem solved, right? Wrong. For many Puritan ministers, the Half Way Covenant went too far in compromising church purity; for others, the Half Way Covenant didn't go far enough to extend the church's influence.

Solomon Stoddard was in this latter camp, and he developed his own system, a policy that was highly controversial in parts of New England—especially with the influential Mather family in Boston. But Stoddard's solution worked wonderfully in Northampton. Under his guidance, Northampton's standards for full church membership were lenient. Anyone who was apparently moral, theologically orthodox, and willing to submit to the church's authority was qualified to join. Furthermore, these people were not halfway members; they were full members, with all the privileges and responsibilities of full membership, including access to the sacraments. Most citizens of the town could meet Stoddard's "open Communion" standards of membership, so the church would represent a majority of the population and, therefore, maintain its force in the community. Stoddard had no interest in trying to figure out who was truly converted and who wasn't. That was an imperfect science at best, he decided—hypocrites can be quite convincing! But if some of those who joined his church were not truly converted, he wasn't overly concerned. Given time, he believed, by living under the authority of the church, these unconverted people would have the best opportunity to experience God's grace. By

hearing the Word preached and taking the sacraments, God could work with their souls to transform them into true Christians. (And Stoddard certainly did his part; his hellfire preaching produced frequent revivals during his long ministry at Northampton.)

Edwards inherited his grandfather Stoddard's policies when he succeeded him as pastor in Northampton, and for years Edwards followed Stoddard's criteria for church membership. Though privately Edwards disagreed with Stoddard's plan, he kept his misgivings to himself, and while he did, the church operated smoothly. Yet, when Edwards openly voiced his opposition to Stoddard's standards a crisis erupted. Edwards's standing in the church and community went from bad to worse. He tried to turn the tide of public opinion that raged against his position, but the people protested his speaking of the matter publicly. So Edwards turned to his other means of persuasion: writing. He defended his position in a 1749 treatise, *An Humble Inquiry into the Rules of the Word of God, Concerning the Qualifications Requisite to a Complete Standing and Full Communion in the Visible Christian Church.* While proclaiming the highest respect for Stoddard and his ministry, Edwards defended his need to examine for himself and make his own judgment. And when he did, he departed from Stoddard's policies. In Edwards's view, those policies were too lax. And from the perspective of Puritan tradition, Edwards's requirement was not unreasonable. In effect, he wanted to return to the earlier practice of the Puritan tradition, requiring that all applicants for full membership give a profession of faith that could be judged by the church. Like his Puritan predecessors, he argued that full members of the church must be "endowed with Christian grace and piety," which could only be judged properly by "profession and appearance." That is, to be a member of the church, one needed not only to *profess* conversion, but had to *appear* to be converted. And that required the judgment of the church. But while Edwards's more strict requirements were not new for Puritans in general, they were most certainly new to Northampton. There, Stoddard's long ministry conditioned the people to expect the more lenient policies. And in changing the rules, Edwards was opposing a legendary minister and changing the cherished policies of his grandfather.

The Northampton church members raised questions about the timing of Edwards's departure from Stoddard's

policy. After all, Edwards had been their pastor for two decades and had never tried to change Stoddard's time-honored traditions before. Why now? More cynical members accused Edwards of intentionally waiting until Stoddard's son, the influential magistrate John Stoddard, died before renouncing John's father's policies. Would Edwards have been so bold if John Stoddard had been around to oppose him?

In retrospect Edwards was actually quite courageous to oppose Stoddard's views when he did. After all, Edwards's status had been deflated substantially by the "young folks' Bible" fiasco as well as a squabble over his salary. He had to know that he was pushing his luck and that there was a good chance he would fail. But Edwards was moved to action by an urgent concern: the fate of revival seemed to be hanging in the balance. Northampton had fallen from its former glory, and perhaps Stoddard's lax standards for church membership were in part to blame. Perhaps by adopting more stringent standards of church membership, Edwards thought, he could reverse the downward direction of his community's spiritual life.

Quite possibly Edwards's expectations for Northampton were too high. If so, though, it is understandable. After all, Edwards recalled longingly the Northampton he knew at the height of revival success. Why could those days not return? Edwards was committed to the ideal situation—he wanted a powerful church with close ties to civil government, the power needed to reform society. But Edwards's zeal for revival convinced him that the church needed to be comprised of authentic Christians who witnessed to religious affections. Like the first Puritans who traveled to America, Edwards was not willing to sacrifice the church's influence in the community, but neither was he willing to sacrifice the church's purity.

In his *Humble Inquiry,* Edwards attempted to explain his position, and in so doing hoped to win Northampton back to his side. But few in Northampton were interested in reading his treatise; their minds were made up. When he insisted on holding a series of lectures on the controversy, many came from surrounding areas to hear his side of the story, but few local folks attended. It was to no avail. When the local votes were counted, Edwards was dismissed, and on July 1, 1750, he preached his farewell sermon.[6]

The Next Frontier

As with everyone who has lost a job, Edwards, not to mention his wife and ten children, must have been asking, "What next?" Where would Edwards go? He had opportunities, even an offer of a position in Scotland, where he was well known and well liked. But Edwards declined. He and his family stayed in Northampton for about a year (certainly not a comfortable option) before moving not only to a new place but to a new cultural experience. Edwards accepted a position as missionary to the Mohican Indians in Stockbridge, an English mission on the Massachusetts frontier. On the surface this seemed like a strange move. One of the complaints against him in Northampton was that he was an antisocial scholar, too wrapped up in his scholarly pursuits and out of touch with the folks in the pews. If this were the case, how would Edwards fare on the frontier, overseeing the daily activities of Mohicans, many of whom barely knew English and could not begin to contemplate the theological intricacies of his sermons? If we look more closely, however, the move made good sense. Edwards had a family connection to Stockbridge. His uncle, John Stoddard, had believed strongly in the mission and had helped to establish the village. Furthermore,

Edwards had already demonstrated a commitment to missions. Just a few years earlier he had befriended David Brainerd, a well-known missionary to Native Americans who came to live with the Edwardses while suffering from tuberculosis. Brainerd developed strong ties to the Edwards family, and an especially close friendship with daughter Jerusha. When Brainerd died at the Edwards's home, he left behind diaries of his missionary experience. Edwards, even in the midst of conflicts with his church, set aside time to edit and to publish Brainerd's dairies as *The Life of David Brainerd*. And it was this profoundly influential work that became Edwards's most read book, motivating missionaries to the field for over a century.

Yet, though the choice was sensible, Edwards's life on the frontier was indeed stressful. First, there was the demanding task of preaching to people of another culture and language; his old sermons from Northampton would not translate well to Native American congregations. Second and most importantly, Edwards and his family had to deal with the dangers of life on the outer edge of English society. At this time the American frontier was a literal battlefield in the constant struggle between England and France over which empire would dominate North American territories. The French and Indian War began while Edwards was at Stockbridge, and the threat of attack was part of daily life.

As such, war and mission were closely connected, and Edwards was on the front lines of both. The Stockbridge mission was part of England's reaction to the French, who were able to enlist the Native Americans' help in fighting the English. The French military alliances with native peoples resulted, in part, from mission activities. Over the years, French Jesuit missionaries had been much more successful than English missionaries in establishing cordial

relations with the Indians. Unlike the English, French missionaries did not try to seize Native American lands, and they spent more time trying to understand the various cultures. For years this French missionary success had shamed Puritan ministers. Puritans were horrified that France, an archenemy of England and, even worse, a nation controlled by Catholics, had outperformed English Protestants on the mission field. English ministers, including Solomon Stoddard, often said that God judged the English for their lack of success in evangelizing Native Americans, and many considered the violent attacks to be part of that judgment. One of the key ways to end these attacks was to convert the native peoples not only to Protestantism but also to English civilization. So the Stockbridge mission was important for political as well as spiritual reasons.

For seven years at Stockbridge, Edwards was a diligent

missionary who took great care in presenting the gospel in a way that the Mohicans could understand. He worked tirelessly to oversee the daily tasks of running a frontier mission. And yet Edwards's attention to detail at Stockbridge did not hamper his scholarly production. The Stockbridge years were among his most prolific. Though he was on the edge of the frontier, he focused his writing on the cutting-edge intellectual issues of his day. After all, there was in his midst a spiritual warfare. The "age of reason" was in full force, and Edwards remained a vigilant defender of the Calvinist worldview in opposition to modern challengers. Most of all, Edwards diligently kept watch on the menace known as Arminianism, well aware of advances Arminian thought continued to make in New England. Two of his Stockbridge treatises were direct responses to this school's assaults on Calvinism, and the following chapters deal with the pressing issues that captivated Arminians and Calvinists alike: the power and limitations of free will, and the origin and extent of sin in the world.

CHAPTER FOUR

Freedom of the Will?

Few ideas are more sacred to Americans than freedom. The United States, after all, was founded on the idea of liberty. Just a glance at the Declaration of Independence gives us all the evidence we need: liberty is a self-evident truth, God-given and undeniable. When Thomas Jefferson wrote these famous lines in praise of liberty, the Enlightenment was in full force. Jefferson, Washington, Franklin, and their colleagues knew they were living in a new intellectual world, an age defined by liberty. They believed that this new day called for a new nation that would exemplify freedom in all its forms—political, intellectual, even theological.

Jonathan Edwards died eighteen years before Jefferson's Declaration and the Revolutionary War that launched this new national adventure in the name of liberty. Edwards, therefore, was not an American patriot; he was a faithful subject of the British Empire. And yet freedom was already a sacred conviction in his lifetime. Edwards thought a lot about freedom—its various definitions, uses, and implications. As we would expect, Edwards was less involved with debates over the extent of political liberty and more preoccupied with how the Enlightenment's celebration of freedom influenced Christianity. More than anything else, Edwards focused on how freedom's rise coincided with Reformed theology's demise. As British poet Alexander Pope expressed the controversy that surrounded Calvinism in the eighteenth century:

> One thinks on Calvin heav'n's own spirit fell;
> Another deems him Instrument of Hell.[1]

Those enlightened thinkers in the latter category believed Calvinism was not only obsolete but also dangerous—that Reformed theology squelched energizing ideas of human ability and ethical responsibility.

Indeed, in Edwards's day, the challenges to Calvinism were many, and some prominent intellectuals questioned the traditional Calvinist idea of divine providence: that God controls the universe and guides all events. If God controls all events, even our choices, the intellectuals deduced, are we not machines rather than free individuals? Moreover, if choices are not free, isn't morality meaningless? How can we hold people responsible for their actions if they do not freely choose them? If God determines our choices, why should we be praised if we do well? or be blamed if we commit evil acts? And speaking of evil, if God controls all events and determines our choices, shouldn't we blame God for our sins? In fact, shouldn't we hold God responsible for the very existence of evil? Though these challenges were not new, they accosted Calvinism in Edwards's day with renewed vigor.

But let's consider equally difficult challenges from another perspective. If God is not in control of the universe, who or what is? Did the universe develop randomly, by sheer chance? If so, is the universe operated by physical laws, with no intellectual or spiritual power at the helm? In defense of Calvinism, Edwards responded that God rules the universe; the world operates neither by random chaos nor through impersonal, mechanistic determinism. But even though God is in control of all events, including our actions, we are free to choose what we

want—we are not machines—and we are responsible for our choices.

Satisfied? Well, if you think these claims are contradictory, you are not alone. Edwards's opponents vigorously agreed. These critics Edwards called "Arminians," a term mentioned earlier but which requires additional definition here. Arminianism was named after Jacobus Arminius, a Dutch theologian of the sixteenth and seventeenth centuries whose followers criticized Calvinism for neglecting human effort in salvation. By the eighteenth century, "Arminian" was a general label for anyone who thought that Calvinism overemphasized the sovereignty of God while neglecting human integrity and freedom.[2] Catching the wave of optimistic, enlightened views of human ability, ministers from Europe to Boston adopted so-called Arminian views of sin and salvation to give more responsibility and credit to humanity.

Edwards, however, deemed Arminianism a serious threat to Christianity. In his view, the Arminian menace lurked throughout England and New England, constantly threatening to invade even the most trusted ministers and cherished institutions. After Edwards graduated and moved to New York, he learned that even Yale had suffered from an outbreak of Arminianism that some called the "Great Apostasy"; seven Yale men joined the Church of England—a hotbed of Arminianism—and then proclaimed Arminian convictions. Perhaps most shocking for Edwards was the news that his former teacher and Yale rector Timothy Cutler was among those who had "defected" to Arminian views. A couple of years after the "apostasy," Edwards returned to Yale as a tutor and considered it his duty to oppose the trend.[3] Yet, Arminian battles continued.

A few years later, after he had succeeded his grandfather, the great Solomon Stoddard, as pastor in Northampton,

Edwards traveled to Boston to deliver a lecture during the celebration of commencement at Harvard. All eyes were on him, and his lecture title communicated his opposition to Arminian challengers: "God Glorified in Man's Dependence."[4] Edwards's text for the lecture was 1 Corinthians 1:29–31, including Paul's command that "He that glorieth, let him glory in the Lord." Paul's concern, as Edwards observed, was that the people in Corinth did not glorify God; they glorified themselves, congratulating themselves for their great wisdom (no doubt influenced by nearby Athens, a leading center of scholarship in the ancient world). Edwards's parallel between his Boston and Paul's Corinth was clear—in both places God's wisdom and grace was neglected in favor of human intelligence and virtue. In response, Edwards argued that sinful humans have no

cause to glorify themselves and are completely dependent on the grace of God. In his precise words, "all the good that they have is in and through Christ." But Edwards knew that more often the eighteenth-century motto of salvation was not "God glorified in human dependence" but "people glorified in their own independence." In his mind, the primary culprits in the corrupting influence were the Arminian "doctrines and schemes of divinity" that rejected "an absolute, and universal dependence on God," and in so doing detracted from God's glory and perverted God's plan of salvation. Instead of "an entire dependence on God" for salvation, Arminians agreed only with "a partial dependence on the power of God" because they wanted to give credit to human free will. In Edwards's view, this "scheme of divinity" robbed God of God's proper glory and left humans with a false sense of security in their own virtues. And he believed the results were catastrophic: these teachings deluded people with visions of self-sufficiency and blinded them to their guilt for sin and the hell that awaited them.[5]

Most of all, Edwards worried that Arminian theology worked against revivalism. Where the latter relied completely on God's transformation of the heart, the former built humans' confidence in their own abilities. Arminianism was an antirevival state of mind—a serious problem for those, like Edwards, who believed that revivals were one of God's primary means of operation in the world. Ironically, in eighteenth-century England and in nineteenth-century America, many of the champions of revival *were* Arminians! The explosion of the Methodist movement is a prime example. Edwards knew that some Arminians advocated revival, but he feared that the Arminian confidence in human abilities would hamper true revival success in the end.

Freedom of the Will: An Edwards Classic

While Edwards faced the Arminian challenge to some degree in his preaching and writing on revival, he attacked Arminianism full-on in his classic *Freedom of the Will.* Published in 1754 while Edwards was a missionary to American Indians in Stockbridge, Massachusetts, *Freedom of the Will* represents the culmination of his years of thought, writing, and preaching on the sovereignty of God in relation to human abilities, especially in reaction to attacks posed by Arminianism. The result is a treatise that impressively defends Reformed theology against challenges from three British authors: Thomas Chubb, Daniel Whitby, and Isaac Watts. Perhaps most radical of the three, Thomas Chubb was a deist in England who never held a ministerial position. Daniel Whitby, however, was an Anglican minister; he had attacked traditional Calvinism in his *Discourse on the Five Points,* published in 1710. Closer to Edwards's theological position, Isaac Watts supported revival and wrote many famous Christian hymns, including "Our God, Our Help in Ages Past," "When I Survey the Wondrous Cross," and the Christmas classic "Joy to the World! the Lord Is Come." We can see, therefore, that Arminianism attracted ministers and thinkers from various backgrounds and perspectives, all united by their complaints against the Calvinist assault on human freedom.[6]

The full title of this work indicates Edwards's central points. Ready? Here it is: *A careful and strict enquiry into The modern prevailing Notions of that Freedom of Will, Which is supposed to be essential To Moral Agency, Vertue and Vice, Reward and Punishment, Praise and Blame.* As long as it is, the title clarifies that the cherished modern idea of freedom was indeed at stake, but so was morality itself. If the will is not free, modern critics argued, then morality is nonsense and people cannot be praised for virtue or blamed for any sins or crimes they commit. Edwards's treatise, therefore, directly engaged Arminian claims on several fronts, involving a psychological state-ment on the nature of the will, an ethical discussion of jus-tice and human agency, and a theological case for God's control in relation to human actions. It has four parts, each critical to Edwards's case for Calvinism. First, he defined often-used terms such as "the will," "necessity," and "inability"—concepts that were essential to the discussion. Second, he tested the Arminian idea of freedom to deter-mine its logical and practical validity. Third, he took on the ethical challenge, evaluating the Arminians' claim that their idea of freedom was necessary to morality. And fourth, Edwards responded to specific claims Arminians made to defend their views. In each section he quoted from his opponents' works, refuting them with counterarguments from Scripture and reason, and in the process assembled a

case that he considered crucial both to the intellectual status of Christianity and to the spiritual progress of revival.

Where There Is a Will There Is a Way . . . But What Is the Best Way to Understand the Will?

Edwards defined the will as our ability to make choices, our power to prefer one option over another and to do what we want. When we choose, we are not indifferent; we are inclined in one direction or another. In discussing the will, just as in discussing religious affections, Edwards emphasized the inclinations, the human power to be inclined rather than in a state of neutrality. When we act on our inclinations we are "willing"—choosing to do something that we want. Whatever our choices happen to be— whether they are deeply pondered choices such as the decision to be a Christian or mundane choices such as the decision to eat a brownie—we choose according to our inclinations and affections. We are able to choose what pleases us, and that power to choose is the will.

Another key term for Edwards is motive, which he defined as anything that "moves, excites or invites the mind" to choose. Recall here Edwards's point in *Religious Affections* about how our psyche is not divided into autonomous powers. The mind is not separable from the inclination, for instance. Instead, when we act, all our powers work together—mind, inclination, affections, and will. This was a very modern view of our subjectivity; some say Edwards is even similar to Freud here.[7] So when Edwards wrote that the motives "excite" us to choose, he means that the motives influence the whole person. Granted that motives are often mixed, making some choices difficult. In these dilemmas Edwards argued that we always choose the option that motivates us most strongly, the option that appears most attractive to us. So while the decision-making process is often obscure, Edwards said that we can count on one constant truth: we always choose what appears most favorable to us. Or, as he said it, "The will always is as the greatest apparent good is."

Particular cases are often complicated, however, especially when we try to determine what "the greatest apparent good" really is in a given scenario. Consider Edwards's example of a "drunkard" who has a bottle in front of him and a decision to make: will he drink the liquor or not? This could be a difficult choice. While drinking would ease the pain of the moment, the pain could be worse in the long run. We can speculate about the worries the drunkard may have about drinking—perhaps a hangover in the morning, continuing a downward spiral into addiction, or dealing with the consequences of any bad decisions he makes while intoxicated. But whatever his choice, the drunkard will choose the option that he believes is his "greatest apparent good" at the time. If he chooses to drink, we'll know that his strongest motive was the desire for instant gratification. If he chooses not to drink, we'll know that his strongest motive was to avoid the painful repercussions of drinking.[8] In effect, therefore, our motives and our decisions reveal what we value most, our greatest good. As Edwards wrote elsewhere, "We mean nothing else, by Greatest Good, but that which agrees most with the inclination or disposition of the soul."[9]

Given the power of his motives, is it accurate to say that the drunkard is free in making his choice to drink? If our choices are determined, even by motives, are we really free? Edwards's Arminian opponents argued that we are only free if our wills are completely undetermined, totally unlimited, and open to any possibility. Ridiculous, said Edwards. Common sense shows us that our wills are never completely open to a universal variety of options. Our wills are limited. After all, what is a motive if not a determination of the will? We will what we want, to be sure, but a motive drives our choices. Our motives determine our choices, and what informs our motives but our inclinations and our "habits and dispositions of the heart"? And remember, Edwards talked about how only God can change the heart? So God is in control, but we are still free because we choose what we want. Our choices are our own.

So Edwards insisted that even though the will is free, it is also determined. We are free to choose what we want even while our motives and inclinations make some choices necessary and other choices impossible. How, we may ask, is this possible? After all, if some choices are necessary, then the will is not free. Edwards resolved this apparent contradiction by distinguishing between "natural necessity" and "moral necessity." Natural necessity on the one hand applies to the natural world, including the laws of math and physics; for example, two plus two always equals four and

YOU ARE QUITE DETERMINED...

parallel lines never intersect. Natural necessity limits our free will. I may want to soar though the air by flapping my arms, but since I do not have natural powers to fly, I will never leave the ground. I have free will, but my desire to fly does not overcome my physical limitations. My freedom is not unlimited, therefore; it is bound by natural laws, and these laws are not negotiable, no matter how strong my desires may be.

"Moral necessity" works in a similar way. Natural forces such as gravity limit our choices, but so do moral forces such as motives and inclinations. Just as we are naturally unable to fly (without mechanical assistance), we are morally restricted from making decisions that go against our strongest motives and inclinations. Edwards illustrated the point with several scenarios. "A woman of great honor and chastity" may be morally unable to become a prostitute, for example, or a "malicious man may be unable to" love his enemies. Does this mean that the chaste woman and the malicious man are not free? No—they are free to do as they want, which is the very definition of freedom. But are their choices determined? Yes—their motives and inclinations guide and limit their decisions. In this way, Edwards argued that freedom is perfectly consistent with determination of the will.[10]

To further clarify the distinction between natural and moral necessity, Edwards told the story of two men who were imprisoned for offending their ruler. After some time passed, the king gave the men a chance at freedom, announcing that the prisoners could be free if they admitted their crimes, vowed to do no more wrong, and pleaded for the king's forgiveness. If the prisoners did what the king asked, the king would not only free them but award them with honorable titles and generous salaries. Given this offer, consider two scenarios. The first prisoner con-

ceded to the king. He bowed before his majesty, pleaded for mercy, and vowed to be a good citizen from then on. And yet, for whatever reason, the doors did not open and the man stayed confined within the bars of his cell. In this scenario, the man was willing to do the good thing, but his will was confined by his physical situation, so he was unable to claim his freedom. This story illustrates Edwards's view of *natural necessity*—the prisoner was physically unable to do what he wanted. This man was *not* free because he was compelled to remain imprisoned.

In contrast, consider the situation of the second prisoner, a proud man who harbored bitter animosity toward the king. He felt no remorse for his crimes, and bowing before his majesty was the last thing he would ever do. In this case, however, the king made an extra effort to free the prisoner; he went to the prison and had the cell unlocked so that no physical barrier stood in the way of the man and his freedom. All he had to do was bow before the king and repent of his wrongdoing, and he could walk out the door. But the prisoner refused to do so. Despite the king's kind offer of deliverance, the prisoner scoffed at the king and remained in his cell. He would rather rot in prison than humble himself before the king. This story illustrates Edwards's view of *moral necessity*. While the cell door was open and the man was physically free to go, he was just as bound to his cell as the man in the first case, who was locked behind brick walls and steel bars. In this case we see, as Edwards wrote, that "a man's evil dispositions may be as strong and immovable as the bars of a castle." But it is not correct to say that the man in the second case was not free. He was able to do the right thing; the problem is that he was not willing to do it. Repenting of his sin and humbling himself before the king was not pleasing to him, so he could not will it.

In this scenario, both men's actions were confined by necessity, but were they both equally guilty? No. The first man's inclinations were good but he was not able to choose the good because of natural necessity. He was not free. The second man's inclinations were evil, but he was free to follow those inclinations and he did. He freely chose to remain incarcerated, even though he was not bound by any physical confinement.[11] This story illustrates the important distinction between "compulsion" and "determinism." If actions are *compelled*, then they are not free. That is, the first prisoner wants to leave his cell but he is not able to do what he wants because the bars of his cell compel him to remain confined. However, acts that may be *determined* can still be free. The case of the second prisoner illustrates this point. He is not compelled to remain in prison: the gates are open and he is physically able to leave. But he remains confined because he is unwilling to leave. His motivation never to obey his king *determines* his will.[12]

Arminian "Free Will"—Uncommitted, Undetermined, and Neutral

The problem, in Edwards's view, was that Arminians perverted a true and commonsense understanding of freedom. The clear meaning of freedom is our ability to do as we want—to choose according to our preferences. If we can choose what we want, we are free, even though our motives and inclinations determine our choices. But Edwards accused Arminians of perverting this understanding of freedom in several ways. First, the Arminian brand of freedom required the will to be a "self-determining power," the ultimate master of human choice, free to act without "any cause outside itself" whatsoever. Second, Arminians believed that the will is not free unless it is in a state of indifference before it acts. If the will is in any way inclined in one direction or another before a decision, then

91

the will's decision is determined and, therefore, not free. Third, they contended that freedom was meaningless unless the will is free of any "necessity, or any fixed and certain connection with some previous ground or reason of its existence." Edwards denied that these three criteria were essential to freedom or morality. Indeed, he argued that these three criteria would render human agency and virtue meaningless.[13]

One of Edwards's main frustrations with the Arminian argument was the common phrase "freedom of the will." Ironically, even though the phrase is commonly used as the abbreviated title of his treatise, Edwards disliked it. To Edwards's mind, the phrase implied that the will is a free agent that has the power to act. Consider for instance the claim of Arminian theologian and brilliant hymn writer Isaac Watts: "The will determines itself in a very sovereign manner," exercising "its own perfect power of choice, ris-

ing from within itself, and free from all influence or restraint of any kind." In other words, the will has the ability to operate with no motive at all. Most likely Edwards would have preferred that Watts had put more energy into composing hymns and less on debating the will![14] To Edwards, this idea was absurd. How can the will itself have freedom? The will is not an autonomous faculty separate from the mind. The will is our power to choose; but the will doesn't choose, we do. Consider his allusion to our capacity to love. "When we say, love seeks the object loved" we mean that "the person loving seeks that object." To use another illustration, a bird can fly, but the bird's power of flying does not itself have the ability to fly. Similarly, our will does not have the freedom to will—we do. Edwards insisted that the will, therefore, is not an independent power. Rather, the will acts in cooperation with other powers of the mind, including motive, inclination, and affection. Recall here Edwards's argument in *Religious Affections* in which he denied the common separation of "head" and "heart," claiming instead that the affections are part of the mind—intellect and affection act together. Likewise here, Edwards opposes stark divisions between warring "departments" of the psyche—the will is not an independent, self-acting power.

Another problem Edwards had with the Arminian view was even more basic. Common sense tells us that nothing exists without some cause or combination of causes; the relationship between cause and effect is a fundamental principle of the natural world. If we cannot assume a connection between cause and effect, we will be helpless to explain the existence of anything from headaches to earthquakes. No human event or power completely determines its own existence. But if the concept of the independent and free will is true, what causes the will to act? Arminians answered that the will causes itself to act, that the will is completely self-determining, because if anything deter-mines the choices of the will, then the will is not free. But in the real world how would the will *cause itself* to act? We would have to conclude that every act of the will is caused by a previous act of the will. So that in order for the will to act, the will would need to will itself to act. As Edwards expressed it, "If the will determines all its own free acts, then every free act of choice is determined by a preceding act of choice, choosing that act."

Edwards was a great lover of chocolate, so let's consider an example he would have appreciated. Let's assume that I am an Arminian with a sweet tooth. I am standing at the bakery counter and I choose to eat a brownie, but it is not that simple. Before I can choose a brownie, I must choose to choose a brownie. After all, something

must cause me to choose a brownie, but it cannot be anything outside of my free will. Before I can choose to choose a brownie, therefore, I must make a previous choice that allows me to choose to choose a brownie! Confused? (Well, other than the fact that you yourself probably now want a brownie.) Edwards thought this was ludicrous too. Obviously such a train of choices could go backward forever. At some point, Edwards concluded, the will, like every other form of reality, must have an external cause. The only exception he made to this rule was God. Only God is self-causing and self-creating—the only fully autonomous agent in the universe.

Simple enough, right? Everything that happens has a cause. Ever the intellectual on the cutting edge, Edwards was well familiar with Newton's explanation of the physical world as a series of causes and effects. Nothing exists outside this universe of causation—there are no uncaused or self-caused occurrences. And yet he believed Arminians were ignoring this basic assumption in their bizarre claims that the will can cause itself. If we give up the idea that everything has a cause, all evidence for any action or being disappears. Consider, for example, arguments for the existence of God. How can we prove that God exists, Edwards wondered, if we cannot reason that the creation is evidence of a creator? Edwards marveled that this commonsense assumption about cause and effect was lost on Arminians.[15]

Free Will and Morality: Debating Virtue, Vice, Praise, and Blame

One of the most serious charges Arminians leveled against Calvinism was this: If the will is determined in any way, then morality itself makes no sense. They argued that if our choices are determined, how can we be praised if we do

well? And how can we be blamed if we commit evil acts? If the will is determined, we can no longer admire saints who sacrifice their lives in service to the poor. Nor can we condemn mass murderers who commit some of history's worst atrocities. If the will is not free to choose either good or evil, the world degenerates into chaos and human agency is lost.

Edwards revealed a major flaw in this argument with one simple question: What about God? If, as the Arminians insisted, freedom requires that the will be absolutely undetermined and neutral, then even God is not free. After all, Edwards wrote, "God is necessarily holy, and his will necessarily determined to that which is good." By nature, God cannot commit an evil act. Therefore, if we agree with the

Arminian view, not only is God not free, but God does not deserve our praise. Edwards delighted in this point because it demonstrated how ludicrous the Arminian position was. And it supports Edwards's argument about human freedom: just because choices are determined does not mean they are not free. We are free if we are able to do what we want, even though our free choices are necessarily determined by our motives. Regardless of what causes us to act, we are able to do what we want. And because we are free to do what we want, we are responsible for the morality of our choices. If we make good choices, we deserve praise; if we make evil choices, we deserve punishment. Contrary to the Arminian claim that Calvinism ruined free will and morality, Edwards responded that the Arminian view of freedom destroyed any concept of the moral life.

Let's look at a biblical example from one of Jesus' well-known parables, revised and updated to illustrate the Arminian view of freedom. A Samaritan is walking on the road from Jerusalem to Jericho when he encounters a man who has been beaten and left to die in the ditch. The Samaritan is free either to help the man or to leave him to die. And because the Samaritan is a free, enlightened thinker, he is not inclined one way or another, but is totally indifferent. To help him decide, he chooses a coin from his purse, flips it, and lets the result of the toss make his decision: heads he helps the man, tails he doesn't. It just so happens that the poor, beaten man is in luck: the coin lands on heads, and the Samaritan comes to his aid, bandaging his wounds and finding him a place to stay. Even though the Samaritan helped the man, should we praise him? Maybe—after all, he did a good thing, whether he wanted to or not. But should we consider him virtuous for helping the man? I don't think so. Do you? He did not do the right thing from the goodness of his heart. Instead, he was

indifferent. He would have been just as satisfied to leave the man in the ditch and go on his way.

Hopefully this illustration illuminates Edwards's point. We do not consider people virtuous if they do the right thing out of indifference. In fact, the opposite is true: the farther from indifference people are, and the more inclined they are to goodness, the more we praise them. We assign blame in the same way. The more intentional and devoted criminals are to their evil acts, the more we condemn them—not only for their individual crimes, but for the corrupt state of their minds. Thus, Edwards concluded that if we follow the Arminian view of freedom, "virtue and vice are wholly excluded out of the world," and there can never be "any such thing as one or the other; either in God, angels or men."

And he further pressed the point, arguing that the modern idea of freedom of the will would make all moral rules meaningless. Moral rules function by guiding our actions, directing us to live in a certain way. In effect, then, ethical regulations destroy the indifference that Arminians require in any free act. If freedom is indifference, as the Arminians claim, moral laws violate the essence of liberty. What about the many pages of moral commands in the Bible? Do they invite us to make free choices about right and wrong, without influencing us? Of course not—biblical rules such as the "Thou shall not" statements in the Ten Commandments combat indifference and strongly direct our decisions. Indifference may be necessary to freedom for Arminians, but indifference is hardly a virtue in Scripture, Edwards asserted.

Though the treatise on the will was philosophically sophisticated, Edwards believed that nothing supported his argument more than ordinary good sense. If we accept the Arminian understanding of freedom, he argued, common sense ideas of freedom, morality, and virtue become meaningless. The problem was that Arminians had confused the issues with "metaphysical and philosophical subtleties" that made no sense in the real world. In contrast, Edwards turned to the understanding of "common people" whose minds were not "perverted from their natural channel" by Arminian confusions. Ordinary people understood that freedom meant simply the ability to do what we want, regardless of any determination of our choices by motive or inclination. Moreover, common people do not believe freedom requires neutrality or indifference. We all know that we choose according to our preferences, guided by our inclinations and motives. And we are not neutral and detached in our actions. We are involved, and our choices are our own.[16]

Divine Sovereignty or Omnipotent Human Will?

Edwards's argument on the will is intricate and involves much more analysis than this chapter reveals. But in reflecting on some of the main issues, consider again the full title of Edwards's treatise: *A careful and strict enquiry into The modern prevailing Notions of that Freedom of Will, Which is supposed to be essential To Moral Agency, Vertue and Vice, Reward and Punishment, Praise and Blame*. Edwards set out to refute the prevailing modern idea of free will as a sovereign human ability, an independent, self-creating power that could resist the strongest motive and even defy the will of God. In Edwards's view, we can believe in either a sovereign human will or a sovereign God, but not both. He argued that the "modern" concept of free will rejected God's rule in human affairs and thwarted God's moral order of the universe. As you now know, the Arminians charged that if God determines all events, morality is a sham. But if God does not control all, who or what does? The answer from most enlightened thinkers was clear: we do. Edwards viewed this claim as an enlightened defense of human control in defiance of divine authority. So Edwards defended the Calvinist position from Scripture (as we would expect a Reformed theologian to do). But his analysis concluded that the Arminian notion of free will was not only unbiblical, but unreasonable—a confused, metaphysical speculation that violated common sense.

If Edwards was correct that the Arminian understanding of free will was unfaithful to Scripture and incompatible with common sense, why was it so popular, even in New England? He addressed this question in a letter to his Scottish friend John Erskine in 1757. In the letter, Edwards admitted that the Arminian idea of free will had one undeniable attraction: it encouraged people to avoid responsi-

bility for their sin. If we can be held accountable for bad decisions only if they are freely chosen with wills that are self-determined and indifferent, then our list of sins is encouragingly short. How often are we indifferent when we sin? Very rarely. In almost all cases we sin not because we are indifferent, but because we want to sin. Our motives are sinful and we choose them; our inclinations are sinful and we follow them. The plain and discouraging truth, Edwards showed, is that our natures are corrupt, our hearts are sinful, and therefore we sin. If that is the case— if we sin because we are inclined toward evil—are we responsible for our sins? Arminians said no. Edwards said yes.

Not surprisingly, freedom of the will was much more than an academic debate for Edwards. Real lives were at stake. The devoted pastor worried that numerous souls would be deceived into damnation by trusting in their freely chosen goodness rather than the grace of God. In order to defeat the Arminian challenge, therefore, Edwards not only had to correct what he believed were Arminian misrepresentations of freedom; he also had to defend traditional claims about human sin. In the final treatise that he finished before his death, he did just that: he took on the Arminian challenge to human depravity and cast new light on what many believed was the most unenlightened of teachings: original sin.

CHAPTER FIVE

Original Sin

Today, as in Edwards's day, sin is provocative. The presence of evil is an intellectual conundrum and a heart-wrenching reality. Consider these perplexing questions: Why would a righteous God allow sin to infest the world? What does it mean to be a sinner? Does everyone sin? If so, where did our moral corruption originate? Is sin an inherited trait, a form of diabolical DNA? Or is sin just something we all learn from experts? In Edwards's view, these questions were difficult—so difficult that all the brilliant knowledge of the Enlightenment was utterly useless in answering them. To his mind the only adequate explanation for sin in the world came not from new knowledge, but from an old doctrine: the concept of original sin. But could this be accepted in the modern world? Was this ancient idea convincing in a society captivated by the new and eager to do away with tradition?

With more than a hint of sarcasm, Edwards wrote that he lived in a "happy age of light and liberty." The "age of light" comment was Edwards's reference to the "enlightened" era, when modern intellectuals believed they had "a more inquisitive genius, and a better discernment" than thinkers of any previous time. (Can you still detect the sarcasm?) As he observed in *Freedom of the Will*, this "age of light" was also an age of "liberty." Confidence reigned supreme as modern people claimed the power to control their own destinies, unlimited by any influence, human or divine. With so much confidence in the "light" of new knowledge and the "liberty" of humanity, no wonder so many thought the eighteenth century a "happy age." Optimism was the tenor of the times.[1] Modern thinkers believed that their age was the best in history. Never before had people possessed the potential to be so intelligent, free, and happy.

How would Edwards's Calvinist faith fare in this new world? In contrast to their "happy age of light and liberty," many modern thinkers believed Calvinism contributed to "a gloomy age of darkness and bondage." For them, Calvinism darkened the mind with scholastic superstitions, bound the will with ideas of human inability, and, perhaps most offensively, tainted human dignity with the doctrine of original sin.

The concept of original sin offended enlightened thinkers because it taught that all people were naturally sinful. According to this idea, sin is central to who we are—our very characters are evil. That concept of depravity was enough to put a damper on optimistic times. But even more offensive for critics of Calvinism was the claim that we are sinful because we share in the first sin ever committed: when Adam and Eve disobeyed God in the Garden of Eden. Being labeled a sinner because of one's own bad behavior is bad enough, but being branded a sinner because of humanity's 'original sin' was too outrageous for many modern people to fathom. Where's the justice in this teaching? How can God hold us accountable for sins that we did not freely commit ourselves? Can God punish us for a sinful nature that we inherited? No idea could be more out of step with the times. Where were the light and the liberty, not to mention the happiness?

Edwards admitted that original sin was not a happy doctrine. It was pessimistic and disturbing—even terrifying. But it was also realistic, biblical, and essential to saving humanity from eternal destruction. Despite its difficulties, Edwards believed that the doctrine of original sin told the truth about the world; and without it real Christianity would become extinct and the possibilities of salvation would be lost. So again Edwards found himself in the unenviable position of defending traditional theological ideas against attacks from modern thinkers whose thoughts seemed brighter and more promising. But just as he did with *Freedom of the Will*, Edwards in *Original Sin* would defend an old idea in a distinctively new way.

Sinful Debates

Not surprisingly, Edwards had many opponents in his debates about sin. Perhaps the most intimidating was John Taylor, a Presbyterian minister in England. Edwards once referred to Taylor as "that author who has so corrupted multitudes in New England."[2] Taylor attacked the doctrine of original sin in a book that Edwards considered so

threatening that he listed it in the title of his own work: *The Great Christian Doctrine of Original Sin defended; Evidences of it's Truth produced, and Arguments to the Contrary answered. Containing, in particular, A Reply to the Objections and Arguings of Dr. John Taylor, in his Book, Intitled, "The Scripture-Doctrine of Original Sin proposed to free and candid Examination."* Taylor's book was a devastating attack on original sin. And to make matters worse for Edwards, a lot of people actually read it.[3] In fact, Edwards determined that Taylor's book was so influential that "no one book has done so much towards rooting out of these western parts of New England, the principles and scheme of religion maintained by our pious and excellent forefathers . . . and alienating the minds of many from what I think are evidently some of the main doctrines of the gospel" as Taylor's attack on original sin. There could be no doubt that Taylor was a worthy foe, and Edwards diligently fought the intellectual fight because he knew that original sin was not a marginal belief that Christianity could do well without. Pessimistic as it was, the doctrine of original sin was essential to Christianity.[4]

Living as we do in the twenty-first century, we may have lost the sense of urgency that Edwards felt about sin. Perhaps we can understand his meaning best if we consider sin in

relation to something that is greatly feared in our time: terminal illness. Edwards believed that sin was a life-threatening disease that was highly treatable. The problem was that many people stricken with the disease denied their illness and, therefore, refused treatment. Most frustrating of all, sinners denied their illness despite showing many symptoms that clearly revealed the disease. In Edwards's view, sin was a malady that threatened the eternal soul. The only cure was Christ's salvation, but the treatment was effective only when those infected recognized their disease and sought treatment.

This analogy between disease and sin reminds us that we misunderstand Edwards if we lose sight of the pastoral dilemmas that provided the basis for his intellectual work. Edwards was a deep thinker, to be sure, but his intellectual energy was focused on what he considered to be central problems that affected people who could not begin to understand the metaphysical subtleties of his reasoning. The original sin debate, therefore, was not a mere academic tangle that gave Edwards the chance to defeat Taylor. He believed Taylor's thought a threat, an imminent danger to real people in New England.

Edwards sensed that danger growing in Northampton, as indicated by his broken relationship with his church. He was convinced that he lost favor with the people of Northampton in part because of "new, fashionable, lax schemes of divinity, which have so greatly prevailed in New England of late." Two years after Northampton dismissed him, he wrote a letter to his former congregation, seeking to advise them against the troubling ideas that were circulating in their midst. Perhaps he thought they were in special need of the advice since they had not yet hired a minister to replace him! Edwards appended the letter to a long defense of his position in the Communion contro-

versy. Even though Edwards had left Northampton, the
controversy had not ended. His estranged cousin, Rev-
erend Solomon Williams of Lebanon, Connecticut, had
published an attack on Edwards's position in the Communion controversy. In effect, Williams defended Stoddard's position on open Communion and chastised
Edwards for the more strict policies that resulted in his fir-
ing. In response, Edwards urged the people of Northampton to take the advice of their rejected pastor who still
cared deeply for their welfare. Most urgently, he pleaded
with them to see the connection between their open Communion policies and the dangerous "lax schemes of divinity" that were spreading throughout the land, thanks

mainly to Taylor and other freethinkers. The situation was dire, in Edwards's view, because of his concern that the church was engaged in a spiritual warfare with cosmic ramifications. Within the apocalyptic mindset that Edwards shared with most Reformed ministers, the end-times were coming, and the church would face persecution at the hands of Satan's forces. Purity, therefore, was essential so that the church could be prepared to meet Christ. We can see, therefore, that the "lax schemes of divinity" threatened the very survival of the church.

The problem was that Northampton's practice of open communion implied that unconverted people were good enough to be church members. It was likely, therefore, that unconverted people would be part of the church without ever knowing the dreaded sinful state of their souls. After all, none liked to admit their own depravity, their own evil. And few would come to terms with their sin unless compelled to do so. That was the duty of the church in preaching the gospel, which included a realistic view of the sinner. Edwards worried that "lax schemes of divinity" would blind the church to the reality of sin. The results would be disastrous. Sinners would never face the truth about their condition. And, as a result, they would go merrily along without truly being converted. They would not see the reality of their sin until they faced the gates of hell, and then it would be too late. In these ominous circumstances, therefore, Edwards pleaded with Northampton "to take the friendly warning" he gave them and to be on "guard against the encroaching evil."[5]

Edwards realized that Northampton was a local example of an international threat. In his treatise on original sin, he mounted a major defense of the traditional doctrine of sin that he believed was under attack on both sides of the Atlantic.

Making Sense of Sin

The odds were stacked against Edwards. How could he successfully defend a view of sin that most people deplored? What could he do to convince people in an optimistic time that their positive view of themselves was wrong and dangerous? First, he needed to prove that original sin was a rational doctrine that made sense of common experience in the eighteenth century. It was the "age of reason," after all, and his case for sin had to be reasonable if it were to have any chance of turning the optimistic tide of the times. Second, he needed to demonstrate that original sin was truly biblical—so faithful to Scripture, in fact, that any attack on original sin was an attack on Scripture itself. Edwards cited many scriptural passages to make his case. But Edwards knew that proof from Scripture was not sufficient. Taylor quoted the Bible too, and his biblical arguments against original sin seemed to have the tenor of the optimistic times on their side. Edwards marveled at how "enemies of this doctrine" of original sin "*force* the Bible to speak a language that is agreeable to their mind!"[6] So Edwards framed his assault in rational as well as biblical terms. Again, he believed that the Bible and reason agreed, that Scripture was the best expression of good sense, and therefore rational and biblical argument flowed together harmoniously.

As he did in his debate on the will, Edwards introduced his argument with a short definition of the concept under study—this time original sin. In doing so, he posited that two related beliefs are fundamental to the doctrine. First, all of us are sinful by nature; we suffer from "innate sinful depravity of the heart." This idea is closely related to themes we've already discussed in Edwards's other treatises. Remember: in our natural state, our *affections* are

111

misdirected toward worldly loves, not empowered by God, and our *wills* are perverted toward evil. We need our affections to be transformed to follow godly loves and our wills and inclinations directed toward divine motives. But until this redeeming transformation occurs, we are corrupt. Second, this sinful state is nothing new. Humans have been naturally sinful since Adam's first sin, because Adam's first sin contaminated all of his "posterity." This means that Adam's sin is our sin; we are guilty of it, and we will be condemned for it in the final judgment . . . that is, unless Christ saves us. Edwards observed that these two ideas normally go together. Those who believe that all people are sinful usually accept that this sinful nature came from Adam's original sin. Likewise, those who deny that all humans are naturally sinful reject the influence of Adam's sin.[7]

The initial question, therefore, is, Can we demonstrate that humans are naturally depraved and sinful? Opponents of original sin said no, and they cited examples of the good that people do. According to this logic, surely, everyone makes mistakes from time to time, but alongside the sins that people commit are numerous good acts. People are complex. They are sometimes selfish and dishonest and other times generous and honorable. How, then, can defenders of original sin make the claim that the "real" human nature is sinful, when evidence to the contrary exists?

Edwards replied that the issue is not decided by comparing the number of good and sinful acts that people commit. The question is whether or not there is "a prevailing tendency to sin" in all people. Can anyone live a perfect life, completely sinless, totally selfless, and in exact obedience to the Ten Commandments, for instance? For Edwards the clear answer was no. Try as we may, we all sin. But Taylor disagreed. How do we know that everyone sins? No one has examined every individual on earth to determine if sin is truly universal. True, Edwards admitted, but neither he nor anyone he knew had ever reported seeing a sinless person. That evidence, combined with biblical teachings that all people are sinners, should be enough to establish the fact that sin is universal.[8]

But even if we agree that everyone sins, does that mean that our souls are naturally corrupt? Those who denied original sin said no. Sin, they claimed, is not a disease that infects the soul and causes us to sin. Instead, sin is a choice. When we choose to sin of our own free will we corrupt ourselves. We are not corrupt before we choose to sin. This explanation accounts for the presence of sin in the world and upholds belief in human freedom and goodness. We are not naturally evil. We are basically good, but we are also free, and our freedom makes it possible for us to sin.

This explanation sounds good, but does it explain why everyone sins? If sin is a free choice, what are the chances that no one ever avoids sinning? Think of the great variety of people in world history—people who speak countless languages and live in various cultures. And yet not one person avoids sin. It all comes down to probability. It only makes sense that "a steady effect argues a steady cause," Edwards said. There must be a reason, a cause of the sinfulness of all humanity. And the only reasonable explanation for the fact that all people sin is that they must have a natural tendency toward sin that all humans share.

The issue as Edwards expressed it, therefore, is not whether we "perform as many good deeds as bad ones," but whether we have a stronger tendency to "a state of innocence and righteousness, and favor with God; or [to] a state of sin, guiltiness, and abhorrence in the sight of God." If we observe a universal tendency toward sin in our nature, then it is irrelevant that we also do some good deeds. Good works, after all, cannot earn salvation. It is the character of the heart that matters, whether one is inclined toward God or Satan, righteousness or sin.

Consider the illustration of a rickety ship that is not sound enough to cross the Atlantic. Would we call this ship "good" just because it could go most of the way across the ocean before sinking? Obviously not—the ship is useless, because it cannot remain seaworthy long enough to complete the voyage; the fact that the ship could stay afloat part of the way does not make up for its tendency to sink eventually. The same is true for human nature. We are depraved because we inevitably sin, no matter that we occasionally behave morally.

Those who consider all people basically good despite a natural tendency toward sin in Edwards's view do not understand the seriousness of human depravity. Human sin is not just a collection of white lies and innocent goofs. Sin deeply implicates people and separates them from a holy God. Edwards called human sin "odious, and also pernicious, fatal and destructive, in the highest sense," a disease that leads to humanity's "eternal ruin" without exception. Any sin seriously offends God. How absurd, therefore, are the arguments that our deep depravity of soul can be balanced by some good deeds. It is as if a prince would consider that his servant "was not a bad servant, because though sometimes he contemned and affronted his master to a great degree, yet he did not spit in his master's face so often as he performed acts of service." Likewise, could a husband believe his wife was good "because, although she committed adultery" occasionally, "yet she did not do this so often as she did the duties of a wife"? Edwards used these examples to demonstrate how ludicrous it was to claim that human sinfulness against God could be balanced by some good actions.[9]

Who's to Blame for Sin—Adam or God?

The idea of original sin has its problems, and Edwards fielded attacks from several fronts. Even if he had been able

to convince his readers that everyone has a sinful nature, the natural follow-up question was even more difficult: Why are we corrupt? Where did our sinful natures come from? The answer, according to the doctrine of original sin, was that sin began with Adam and Eve in the Garden of Eden. A classic defense of original sin comes from Romans 5, where Paul, writing specifically about Adam, said, "By the one man's disobedience the many were made sinners" (Rom. 5:19 NRSV). Genesis chapters 2 and 3 detail the story of how Adam and Eve disobeyed God by eating fruit from the one tree that God had forbidden them to touch. But the pressing question was, why did Adam sin? This question was especially tricky for Edwards because he argued that sinful acts result from a sinful nature. His *Freedom of the Will* made clear that our actions follow our inclinations. If we are inclined to sin, we sin. We have the freedom to do what we want, and we sin because we want to sin, due to the corruption of our wills. But "in the beginning" Adam's will was not corrupt. How, then, could

Edwards explain Adam's disobedience? If Adam could sin without a corrupt nature, then why can't we?

This was a dilemma for Edwards, perhaps the most troubling issue he faced in defending original sin. He responded that, technically, one sinful act—such as Adam's first sin—does not prove that a person has a "fixed inclination" toward evil. Rather, we know our natures are sinful because we sin repeatedly throughout our lives, and we cannot stop sinning. Consider an illustration. A man who has no desire to drink is tricked by "a pretended friend" to take one drink of liquor. But that first drink arouses the man's desire for liquor, and he becomes an alcoholic. Can we argue that he could have taken the first drink without a strong inclination to drink? Yes—he was deceived into taking the first drink. Only afterward did he develop a strong inclination to drink excessively.

In light of this example, consider Adam's first sin. He did not sin because he had a strong inclination to sin. His motives were not totally depraved. God had established a covenant with Adam and Eve, a covenant based on works. If they obeyed God's divine law, they would be happy and fulfill their purpose of living in communion with God. Adam and Eve were equipped with the ability to honor this covenant. Their natures were not tainted. So Adam, like the man in the previous illustration, sinned not out of a sinful motive, but out of deception. Adam was deceived; consequently, he sinned. Certainly he did not know the disastrous consequences that would result from eating from the forbidden tree. He had no idea that his sin would doom the human race and, as Edwards described, "pave the whole globe with skulls." In short: Satan, in the form of the serpent, deceived Adam, convincing him that only good would result from his disobedience, not disaster.[10] The argument was not Edwards's strongest. Certainly

Adam knew that eating from the tree was against God's commands, so we can hardly conclude that he was completely deceived. And even if he was, is not deception a central component of most sinful choices? Nevertheless, Edwards did offer a plausible account of why Adam could sin without a sinful nature.

Behind the question of Adam's sin was a more serious issue: the role of God in bringing sin into the world. Did God set Adam up to fail? If God and Adam were in such close communion, how could Adam have sinned without God's intervention? If this were the case, then God is "the author" of sin and damnation. Such a God would be unjust and even sadistic.

Edwards argued that this "grand objection" against original sin was baseless. The doctrine of original sin does not teach that God caused anyone to sin. God never implanted

118

any corrupt or evil "infection" in human nature. Granted, God did allow humans to sin, but there is a difference between directly *causing* something to occur and *allowing* it to happen.

As Edwards explained, God created Adam and Eve with two kinds of principles in their souls. First, God created "inferior" principles that are common to everyone, including "natural appetites and passions." Second, God created "superior principles, that were spiritual, holy and divine." In contrast to the natural principles, these were "supernatural" principles. Through these supernatural principles, Adam and Eve enjoyed a close relationship with God, empowered by the Holy Spirit's constant presence in their hearts. And God designed the supernatural principles to reign over the natural principles. In other words, Adam and Eve's relationship with God would be the center of their lives, and all their other needs and desires would be secondary to their love of God.

When Adam sinned, this meticulous design fell apart. And the results were devastating. God's presence departed from the soul, leaving humanity "in a state of darkness, woeful corruption and ruin." The natural principles, which God designed to serve the supernatural principles, took control of the soul and "became absolute masters of the heart," resulting in "a *fatal catastrophe*, a turning of all things upside down" for humanity. In this catastrophic revolution in the soul, natural desires ruled. Edwards compared these natural principles to "fire in an house," which is "a good servant, but a bad master." Confined within a fireplace, a fire is comfortable and greatly helpful to the home, but if the fire blazes out of control it destroys the house.

Thus, Edwards concluded, God is not the author of human depravity. God did not directly cause humans to be sinful; God never polluted the human soul with evil. After Adam's sin, the inferior, natural principles of the human soul rebelled against the superior, supernatural principles, and as a result, God's rule in the human heart ended. God departed, therefore, which was all a holy God could do in the face of evil rebellion. God was "driven away by" humanity's "abominable wickedness," and, as a result, the human soul was left to its own corruption. One could argue that God indirectly caused human depravity by taking away divine influence, but an indirect cause is much different from a direct cause. When I turn off a lamp at night, I do not cause the darkness directly; darkness is the natural state of things at night. I have simply removed the light, which leaves the room in its natural state of darkness. In the same way, Edwards described, God did not cause sin by removing divine influences in the soul; God's removal

of divine influences merely left the soul to its own sinful inclinations.[11]

Conspiring in Eden:
Can We Be Guilty of Adam's Sin?

Lest you begin to think the intellectual problem is solved, even more serious difficulties remained. After Edwards disputed the claim that God corrupted human nature, he had to deal with this: How could God hold all humans accountable for Adam's sin? For many modern critics, this idea was preposterous and offensive. They reasoned that individuals should be accountable for the sins they committed personally, not a sin committed by the first man eons ago. And yet the doctrine of original sin claimed that Adam's sin was "imputed" to all humanity, and all humans are considered guilty of this sin and are liable to be punished for it. And Edwards vowed to demonstrate the reasonableness of the doctrine, in response to the opposition raised by many eighteenth-century thinkers.

In Edwards's view, the perceived problem was not with the doctrine but with modern thinkers who focused too much on the individual. While God certainly deals with individuals, the Bible often describes how God dealt with humans in covenants, social contracts that treat all of humanity as a unit. God entered into a covenant with Adam and Eve. But the covenant was not only with Adam and Eve as individuals; the covenant was with all of humanity—Adam and Eve were the representatives. According to the agreement, humanity was to obey God; in return, God would grant humans eternal life. When Adam and Eve disobeyed God, they broke the covenant, and since they were the representatives of all humanity, the punishment handed down applied to all people.

Edwards illustrated this using the image of a tree: Adam may have been the root of the tree of humanity, while later people were part of the trunk and branches, but they were all one organism. If the roots of the tree become corrupted, the trunk and branches suffer. Adam's corruption, therefore, had to extend to his descendants. They share in the "evil disposition" that was in Adam when he sinned. Edwards admitted that the doctrine was difficult to accept, but responded that we should "get over the difficulty" in part by realizing that our minds cannot make sense of all divine mysteries. But critics claimed that the doctrine was not only unjust but false, because it did not pass the test of human experience. How can my identity be connected with Adam to the extent that his sin can be identified with me? I am an individual, after all, as was Adam. What connects us in such a way that his guilt can become mine?

Edwards found the answer in the nature of human identity. Again, he uses the image of a tree to make his point. Consider a large tree that is over a century old. This tree looks nothing like the tiny "sprout, that first came out of the ground, from whence it grew," and yet the sprout and the tree are one plant, even though they are materially quite different. The same is true of a forty-year-old man. Thirty-nine years before, he looked entirely different—his appearance and physiological composition were quite different, though the man and the baby are one person. What is the essence of the man's identity? Is it material? Certainly not, as the substances of the body completely change over time. And not only are the bodies of the baby and the man essentially distinct, so are their intellectual capacities, memories, and overall understanding of themselves. Edwards's solution was that God determines identity and preserves it over time, connecting past and present. And this process explains how we share the taint of Adam's sin. God treats

humanity as a whole, not isolated individuals only. When Adam sinned, therefore, God identified all humanity with that sin. So when each person is born, part of that person's identity is sin, which is maintained by God's continued creation. So we share in Adam's fall because *God identifies it with us*; it is a characteristic of all humanity perpetuated throughout history through God's continued process of creation.

In defending this concept, Edwards emphasized that all creation depends on God for its existence. Everything that exists must have a cause, and that ultimate cause is God. Obviously God uses natural causes to create—parents give birth to babies, and acorns produce oak trees, but God creates and uses these natural causes; they don't exist or have creative power on their own. According to Edwards, nothing exists unless God creates it. And nothing continues to exist without God's preservation. Edwards illustrated this idea in his most famous sermon, "Sinners in the Hands of an Angry God," where he preached that just "as one holds a spider, or some loathsome insect, over the fire," God holds sinners over the fires of hell, and it is "nothing but his hand that" prevents them "from falling into the fire at every moment" of life. All existence at each moment is dependent on God's continuing activity. Complicated? Sure. But consider the alternative. Either God is the creator and sustainer of the universe or God is not. If God is the creator and sustainer of everything that exists, then it makes no sense to conclude that God does not keep the

world going all the time, moment by moment. And unfortunately, due to Adam's sin, the creation that God constantly upholds is tainted by evil.[12]

From Original Sin to Virtuous Creation

This connection between morality and creation fascinated Edwards. Each moment, as God continually creates, part of that creation bears the marks of the evil that began with Adam. But this was not God's ultimate goal for creation—far from it. In Edwards's "two dissertations," which we will consider in the next chapter, Edwards connected the goodness and virtue of God with creation. His goal was to demonstrate that God's purpose in creation was to shine forth divine goodness. In response, God intended for humanity to love God above all and to reflect God's virtuous glory.

This vision of "true virtue" as the "end of creation" was much on Edwards's mind when he wrote *Original Sin*. Edwards feared that many people of his time had lost sight of sin in part because they had lost sight of true goodness. There was a growing tendency for people to believe they were naturally virtuous, even without God's help. This sense of natural virtue blinded people to the true virtue that God expects of them—a much higher standard. Tragically, therefore, people went along thinking they were virtuous when in fact they were horribly depraved. Not that all people were committing vicious crimes against humanity. But, more subtly and dangerously, they sinned not by evil actions but by failing to live virtuously, not meeting the biblical expectation to love God above all other desires. Consider Edwards's observation that if our esteem of God, our desire for God, and our delight in God were what they should be, they would "exceed our regard to other things, as the heavens are high above the earth, and would swallow up all other affections, like a deluge."[13]

Tragically, humans have never come close to loving God to this extent. Human depravity is this failure to love God as God deserves to be loved. Edwards's hope was that, with the help of his *Original Sin*, people would recognize the extent of their sinfulness, seek God, and receive holy redemption. Only then could they experience the true virtue that was at the center of God's design in creating the world.

CHAPTER SIX

Creation and True Virtue

By the time Edwards sent *Original Sin* to the press he had already drafted *The End for Which God Created the World* and *The Nature of True Virtue*. Like *Freedom of the Will* and *Original Sin*, Edwards's works on creation and virtue attacked the "fashionable scheme of divinity" that plagued Reformed Christianity in the age of enlightenment. Edwards did not live to send these two dissertations to press, but he planned to publish them together because each depended on the other. In *The End for Which God Created the World*, Edwards dealt with the meaning of creation itself. Here he asked monumental questions such as "Why did God create the universe?" And, more specifically,

"Why did God create humanity?" These are deep, philosophical questions, but for Edwards they were also practical. Once we know our place in God's creation, we will know how we should live in relationship to God, and that was the topic of *The Nature of True Virtue*. In it he described the virtuous life that results when believers are transformed by God. By combining a treatise on God's purpose in creation with a treatise on human life lived in response to God's glory, Edwards unveiled a compelling analysis of God's creation and its intimate connection with the virtuous life.[1]

Creation and the Glory of God

Why did God choose to create? This question was tricky for Edwards. After all, in treatise after treatise and sermon after sermon, he repeatedly defended the absolute sovereignty of God. And if Edwards was correct in his view that God

was ultimately sovereign and self-sufficient, lacking nothing and needing nothing, then what was God's ultimate purpose in creating a universe? Since God did not *need* to create, God must have *wanted* to create the universe. Why? Edwards reasoned that God must have created the universe to glorify God. We may respond that this kind of God would be arrogant and self-centered. But consider Edwards's logic. If God did not create for his own sake, what other purpose was worthy of such divine action? Humanity, perhaps? As we have observed, many thinkers in Edwards's day believed that humans were the center of the universe. (*Now* who was being arrogant and self-centered? Edwards asked.) As a good Calvinist, Edwards dismissed outright this grotesque example of human pride. Certainly fallible humans were hardly worthy to be God's ultimate purpose in creation. For something to be worthy to be God's ultimate purpose in creation, it had to be the highest possible goal that creation could attain. Edwards concluded, therefore, that only God was worthy to be the center of the universe, and the best that creation could aspire to would be to magnify God's glory.[2]

Without creation, Edwards reasoned, God would have had no opportunity to exercise God's holy attributes; in Edwards's words, God's power would "forever have been dormant and useless," and "divine wisdom and prudence would have had no exercise" in any way.[3] In creation, therefore, God exercised divine power and displayed his wondrous glory and beauty. In previous chapters we have discussed Edwards's embrace of nature as a vast communication of God's glory. From the meticulous dexterity of a spider spinning a web to the awe-inspiring beauty of the moon and the stars, the universe reflects the excellence, harmony, and beauty of God. As Edwards observed in the title of a notebook discussed in a previous chapter, he saw in all the excellence of creation "Images of Divine Things." Just as he wrote in that early notebook, so he wrote thirty years later in his *End for Which God Created the World*: God designed the world to "exhibit an image of himself," the creator.

In creating the world, however, God did not display God's handiwork only for self-adoration. What a shame it would be if God's glorious power and attributes were unknown and uncelebrated! Edwards reasoned that it was only right "that the glorious perfections of God should be known, and the operations and expressions of them seen by other beings beside himself."[4] So God created humanity with a special capacity to glorify God and commune with God. If God had not created humans, God's relationship with creation would have been severely limited. Granted, God could reveal much of the divine excellence in the physical world—in the beauty of a sunflower or the power of a thunderstorm, for instance. But Edwards observed that God's highest form of beauty was moral excellence, a special form of God's beauty and goodness that only a creature with moral sensibilities could appreciate. Here Edwards pictured God as "an infinite fountain of holiness, moral excellence and beauty," constantly overflowing from God to humanity.[5] Only humans had the capacity to perceive the goodness of God and to respond by loving and delighting in God above all else. And when humans commune with God in this way they please God and fulfill God's plan for them in creation.

But again Edwards here entered potentially difficult territory. He asserted that our praise pleases God. But does this mean that God *needs* our praise or approval? Edwards's response was a firm "no." God is fully complete and perfect, lacking nothing, so God needs nothing that we can give of ourselves. In fact, as creatures, we depend totally on

God for all that we are and have, so there is nothing that we can contribute to God from our own power. So where did that leave Edwards? He solved the problem by arguing that when we praise God, we please God not by giving God something that belongs to us, but by reflecting God's love and glory back to God. Like a jewel, which is beautiful not because it has any light of its own but because it reflects "the sun's brightness, though immensely less in degree,"[6] in loving God with all our being we glorify God by reflecting God's love to God and to others.

So much for Edwards's reputation as a dour Calvinist who reveled in hell and misery. Instead, God's beauty and excellence captivated Edwards. He longed for a joyous world filled with Christians who celebrated the divine goodness that empowered all of creation. It is true that Edwards did not believe that human happiness was the

goal of creation, and on this point he disagreed with the philosophical trends of his time. Still, God wants us to be happy, said Edwards, and our true happiness "consists in rejoicing in God" above all.[7] We are truly happy when we are "united to God in love," when our hearts are "drawn nearer and nearer to God, and the union with God becomes more firm and close."[8] Edwards summarized the point nicely: "As all things are from God as their first cause and fountain; so all things tend to him, and in their progress come nearer and nearer to him through all eternity: which argues that he who is their first cause is their last end."[9] And that, to Edwards, is the ultimate purpose of creation.

Some may object that a God who creates humans just to receive their praise is a selfish God. Wouldn't a more benevolent God put human happiness first and be less concerned with self-glory? Not from Edwards's perspective. He explained that true happiness is inseparable from the

glory of God. Humanity was created to glorify God, to live in communion with God, and humans are truly happy only when they fulfill this purpose. So God created the universe primarily to increase God's own glory, but human happiness was an essential part of that purpose. The celebration of God and the happiness of humanity are inseparable.[10]

So while God was the center of the universe, this did not mean that humanity was a frivolous experiment in God's laboratory of creation. Far from it. Though God's ultimate purpose in creating the world was to glorify God, humans were central to that great creative effort. Of all God's creatures, only humans had the capacity to truly glorify God. Humans achieved this great cosmic goal by reflecting the beauty of God's moral excellence. So for Edwards, God's ultimate purpose in creation involved the human ability to live lives transformed by divine virtue. The natural supplement to *The End for Which God Created the World*, therefore, was Edwards's *Nature of True Virtue*. Edwards was keenly aware that the term "virtue" was quite loaded in the eighteenth century. Most of all, Edwards recognized that his understanding of virtue differed significantly from the view of virtue that was in vogue in the prominent moral philosophy of the eighteenth century. If "virtue" was central to God's ultimate purpose in creation, then Edwards had to show how the authentic virtue that had such cosmic importance was far different from the limited virtue that reigned in the Enlightenment.

God's Beauty in the World: Creation and Virtue

Edwards's *Nature of True Virtue* struck at the heart of modern ideas about morality. Such an attack on modern moral thought was needed, Edwards believed, because the moral philosophy that was gaining popularity threatened to

undermine the Christian foundations of the moral life. In particular, moral philosophers rethought the traditionally close relationship between morality and religion. Many of these thinkers had soured on traditional Christianity. As a result, they concluded that the only real value of religion was in its moral teachings. Edwards's famous contemporary Benjamin Franklin was a perfect example. He had little use for religious doctrine. Theology, in his view, was a convoluted system of ideas that few could agree on. Most often, theological conversation turned into debate, which often degenerated into dispute and even violence, as in the European religious wars between Protestants and Catholics in the seventeenth century. Like many of his contemporaries, therefore, Franklin found the value of religion mostly in its practical instruction in virtue. Given the choice, Franklin believed it much more important to be moral than to be pious or orthodox. "A virtuous Heretic shall be saved before a wicked Christian," Franklin once quipped. That is, not only can heretics be virtuous, but their virtue is good enough to qualify them for eternal rewards in the afterlife. The best approach, therefore, was to separate the valuable moral teachings from their doctrinal trappings. In pursuit of this goal, moral philosophers liberated virtue from the control of theology. *The Nature of True Virtue*, therefore, was Edwards's response to thinkers who believed that the highest form of virtue was a natural part of the universe that was accessible to everyone, regardless of whether the person had any concept of God at all.[11]

Not All That Glitters—Distinguishing Virtue from *True* Virtue

The Nature of True Virtue reveals most clearly Edwards's skills as a moral philosopher. Unlike most of Edwards's treatises,

which blended philosophical and theological arguments and included significant exegetical reasoning, *True Virtue* was most purely a philosophical argument with few theological points and no section on biblical arguments. Edwards concentrated on philosophical topics in *True Virtue* because he had already made the theological and exegetical side of the argument in *The End for Which God Created the World*. But in *True Virtue*, Edwards launched a focused attack on the general direction of moral thought in his day. A major representative of the moral vision that Edwards opposed was Francis Hutcheson, a Scottish thinker whose concept of a natural moral sense influenced many intellectuals, all to ill effect, in Edwards's view. Together, *The End for Which* and *True Virtue* opposed the "schemes of morality" represented by Hutcheson and other thinkers. Edwards's goal in these two dissertations was to prove that his opponents were not only theologically negligent, they were philosophically wrong.[12]

Edwards began his description of virtue where Hutcheson and others did: with a discussion of beauty. Virtue, Edwards observed, was a brilliant example of beauty. But unlike "the beauty of a building, of a flower, or of the rainbow," Edwards described virtue as another kind of beauty, even the highest form of beauty in existence. He wrote that "virtue is the beauty of the qualities and exercises of the heart, or those actions which proceed from them."[13] We misunderstand morality if we think of it only as a list of rules and regulations—dos and don'ts that keep us in line. To Edwards, morality reveals the beauty of God's order and justice. So the most crucial ethical question for Edwards was, What "renders any habit, disposition, or exercise of the heart truly *beautiful*?"[14]

While Edwards saw great beauty in the virtuous life, he argued that not all concepts of virtue were equally beautiful. As the title of this dissertation indicates, Edwards was making the case for *true* virtue, which was superior to the virtue in the moral philosophy of Hutcheson and others. Edwards defined true virtue as "benevolence to Being in general" or, more specifically, "that consent, propensity and union of heart to Being in general, that is immediately exercised in a general good will."[15] Clearly this definition is philosophically dense, but it is also important enough to review carefully. To start, Edwards's point is that true virtue is not a selfish love whereby we love ourselves above all. Instead, true virtue is *benevolence*, defined as a selfless desire for the good of another. If I feel benevolence toward a person, for instance, I desire her well-being and happiness regardless of any benefit I may gain from loving her and regardless of whether she is attractive or repulsive. True virtue is also selfless in that it is directed toward *Being in general*. That is, true virtue is directed outwardly toward all that exists (or "Being in general") and not a self-focused love of our own good. Edwards expressed this selfless, outwardly focused love in his statement that true virtue is "exercised in a general good will." True virtue, therefore, is distinguished by its focus on "Being in general, or the great system of universal existence" rather than a more narrow love of "any one particular being, that is but a small part of this whole."[16]

If you think of this kind of philosophical terminology as a sure cure for insomnia, don't worry; Edwards stated his definition more clearly in theological terms. Love to "Being in general" was Edwards's philosophical description of "love to God." Edwards described God as "Being in general" because God is "the Being of beings, infinitely the greatest and best of beings."[17] God has "the greatest share of existence." Simply put, God is enormous in that God has more "being" than anything else. Even the universe itself is small compared to God. It makes sense, therefore, that if true virtue is an outwardly directed love of "being in general," then it will focus on the great majority of existence or "being" in the universe, which is God. Briefly stated, therefore, true virtue consists in loving God above all else.

If we are truly virtuous, however, we love God not only because God is the ultimate "being" in existence; we also love God because of God's incomparable beauty. In *True Virtue* Edwards's ruminations on God's beauty are inspiring. Consider this: "All the beauty to be found throughout the whole creation, is but the reflection of the diffused beams" shining forth from God.[18] And this: God is "the foundation and fountain of all being and all beauty; from whom all is perfectly derived, and on whom all is most absolutely and perfectly dependent." Just as the Sun is the

source of all light, God is the source of all life and beauty.[19] Ponder the images: God as an eternal fountain that overflows with beautiful waters of life; God as the sun that radiates beams of life throughout the universe. They are poetic descriptions indeed.

This awe-inspiring God, the source of universal life and beauty, deserves our heartfelt love; unfortunately for Edwards, most modern moral philosophy neglected this central truth. For all their constant talk of virtue as beauty and excellence, these modern schemes of morality neglected the love of God and focused instead on love of ourselves—"self love" rather than divine love. Edwards did not claim that we are wrong to love ourselves and those connected with us. Of course we should love our families and friends, for instance. Edwards's point was that these are "private affections"—limited to a particular circle of beings who are related directly to us personally, and not extending to all. While Edwards agreed that it was human nature to love those connected directly to us, he argued that true virtue is much broader and deeper than our natural loves. True virtue is a "general benevolence," focused on God and extending forth to "the whole existence" of creation.[20] Love of anything other than God, including family, nation, or even church is not true virtue unless these loves are a secondary extension of our primary love of God. When we love God, our other loves are prioritized and properly aligned. We should love God first of all, and then our love of God will empower our love for others. In contrast, Edwards saw modern moral philosophy as too limited because it taught the love of humanity above all, not the love of God.[21]

Perhaps true virtue is best understood as loving in the same way that God loves. In Edwards's view, this love of God is literally the center of the universe. Consider the

Trinity as the supreme example. God is the ultimate model and source of true virtue because "the virtue of the divine mind" exemplifies "love to himself . . . in the mutual love and friendship" that endures though the "persons in the Godhead," Father, Son, and Holy Spirit.[22] This divine love is dynamic, flowing between the Father, Son, and Holy Spirit, and extending from God to all creation. This is true virtue as displayed in God and reciprocated in creation when all our loves center on loving God supremely. Our minds and activities are truly virtuous when they focus on "love to God" and "above all things seek the glory of God" as our "supreme, governing, and ultimate" purpose in life.[23] Without this perspective on love and life's purpose, we are fundamentally limited.

True virtue, therefore, is a godlike love. As such, true virtue is significantly different from the self-love that comes naturally to us. Edwards insisted on this distinction between the godlike love, which was the essence of true virtue, and natural self-love, which was the basis of common morality. Even so, Edwards acknowledged that natural self-love is not bad in itself. One of the chief benefits of self-love is the *conscience*. In defining the conscience, Edwards agreed with a common view: the conscience is universal and natural for all of us, regardless of any religious convictions we may or may not have. Moreover, Edwards wrote that conscience consisted of two key elements. First, the conscience is our natural awareness that we should live by the Golden Rule, at least in the negative sense; we all know that we should not treat others in a way

that we would not like to be treated. Through our conscience, we know that there should be consistency between how we act toward others and how we want others to act toward us. When we disobey this law of conscience, we are naturally uneasy because we contradict ourselves. Second, the conscience gives us a natural sense of justice. Through the conscience, we instinctively recognize the natural relationship between evil deeds and punishment and between good works and rewards. And when this natural "harmony" is broken, we disapprove, as when we see evil people prosper while good people suffer. No one doubts that conscience is essential to life in the world. When we find just one deranged person who seems to have no conscience, we are shocked. So the conscience is good, in Edwards's view. The problem, however, was that moral philosophers commonly made no distinction between the natural moral sense—the conscience—and the divinely inspired moral sense of true virtue.[24]

How, then, does conscience fall short of true virtue? Why were the moral philosophers that Edwards opposed wrong to suppose the natural conscience was the same as true virtue? Here we recall that conscience, for all its great benefits, is a form of self-love—it concerns our need for a harmony between our treatment of others and the way we want to be treated. This inner harmony is good for us; we desire it because we love ourselves and we naturally hate to be in conflict with ourselves. The inner turmoil of a guilty conscience hurts us, so we naturally avoid it out of a sense of self-love. More importantly, however, Edwards observed that even though the conscience reveals the difference between good and evil, the conscience does not cause us to *love* good and *hate* evil because of our benevolence for all being. In contrast, if our sense of virtue arises from our union with God, we are "loving or hating actions from a sense of the primary beauty of true virtue, and odiousness of sin." We love virtue and hate sin because we see them in their entirety, from a divine perspective, and we react to their beauty and ugliness respectively. Edwards makes the following distinction: while conscience is a natural "sense" that we have of justice, true virtue is "a truly virtuous taste, or determination of mind to relish and delight in the essential beauty of true virtue, arising from a virtuous benevolence of heart."[25] In conscience, we may understand that we are sinning, but that does not necessarily mean that our hearts are changed to hate the sin and repent. A man who commits adultery may know through his conscience that he is doing wrong, but that does not mean that he hates his adulterous affair; he may love his sinful passion even though it is wrong. His conscience may convict him of his sin, but that conviction does not necessarily lead him to hate the sin and love virtue.

Edwards found a chief example in the day of judgment. On that day, God will do as any good judge would—show the evidence against the convicted and demonstrate that they have been justly sentenced to punishment. At this point sinners will see the justice of their damnation, but that does not mean they will become holy lovers of virtue and haters of evil. In fact, the opposite will occur—sinners will become even more defiant in their hatred of good and love of evil, "and wicked men will become very devils" as they are led to damnation. These damned souls may see the justice of their condemnation, but this acknowledgment of justice is quite different from true virtue, which is a disposition to hate evil and to love God "from a view of the beauty of his holiness."[26]

Near the end of his treatise, Edwards discussed why the natural affections and principles that are common to all humanity are often mistaken for true virtue. He posited that the main reason stemmed from both true virtue and natural

virtues being types of love. Systems of morality in the eighteenth century tended toward virtue in this lesser sense, building an entire order of life on human love and not on divine benevolence. This narrow view of morality is tempting because of the human tendency to neglect God in considering life in the world. Instead of honoring God as central to justice and human potential, Edwards believed that many view God "as a kind of shadowy, imaginary being" who has no necessary connection to morality.[27] This view of God haunted Edwards. It was a deity who was increasingly vague, powerless, and disconnected from the world. Edwards encountered this same "imaginary" God in moral debates, and *True Virtue* was Edwards's attempt to oppose the modern effort to usher God out of the moral world. In placing God in the center of morality, Edwards asserted the prominence of true virtue, which surpasses all natural loves in breadth and depth, embracing God and all creation.

It All Comes Together in *The End* and *True Virtue*

In these two dissertations, *Concerning the End for Which God Created the World* and *The Nature of True Virtue*,

therefore, Edwards argued that God was absolutely central to all of life—the one enduring reality in the universe. God created the world to exercise God's divine attributes, including holiness, power, and love. All creation exists to glorify God. We fulfill our reason for living when we glorify God in our lives, allowing God to transform us to reflect true virtue. This cosmic, ethical vision of reality displays many of Edwards's major ideas. As we may expect from a revivalist preacher, conversion is absolutely central in this vision. While sin separates us from God, God's self-revelation allows us to be transformed so that we can be in communion with God. In the process, our inclinations and wills take on divine directions as our affections spring from divine initiatives. But this is not only an inner transformation. As Edwards asserted in *Religious Affections*, a heart transformed by God bears the identifiable marks, "fruits" of God's love in the shape of a virtuous life.

CHAPTER SEVEN

A Legacy Begun
The Edwards Ethos

In 1757, at the age of fifty-three, Jonathan Edwards faced an unexpected challenge. He received an offer to be the third president of the College of New Jersey, forerunner to modern-day Princeton University. However, this opportunity came laced with great heartache. Edwards's son-in-law Aaron Burr, the second president of the college, had died suddenly in his early forties, leaving behind his wife, Esther Edwards Burr, and their two children. Understandably Edwards mulled over the offer with conflicting emotions. In October 1757, he wrote a letter to the trustees of the college to convey his thoughts on the position, his qualifications, and his calling; and if this were a cover letter for a job application, it would have been one of the worst ever written. Edwards began with a list of all the reasons why he was all wrong for the position. First, he doubted that he could see himself in the role of college president. Second, he would have to overcome several logistical issues—he had a large family to move, and they had just recovered from the financial strain of the previous move from Northampton to Stockbridge. Third, his many faults (all "generally known" about him) would clearly prevent him from doing a good job. Most visibly, Edwards's health was weak and his personality was unusual. He had "a constitution in many respects peculiar unhappy" and "a low tide of spirits" that constantly plagued him. Edwards also explained to the trustees—in case they did not know— that college presidents needed to be good speakers and skilled conversationalists, and that, in Edwards's opinion, wasn't him; rather, he had a "childish weakness and contemptibleness of speech, presence, and demeanor," including "a disagreeable dullness and stiffness, much unfitting me for conversation," much less for leading a college. Given these deficiencies, he worried that he would be a huge disappointment to the college if the trustees chose him to replace his son-in-law, a vastly superior representative for the school by comparison.

Then, after listing the reasons why the college should reject him, Edwards turned to the reasons why he might need to refuse them. His main concern was that the responsibilities of college presidency would interrupt the studies that had "swallowed up" his mind and been the "chief entertainment and delight" of his life. For all the hardships of the Stockbridge mission, the work there had at least left him time to write, and he guarded this time for study jealously, not just because he loved it, but because it was central to his calling. Study for him was an urgent matter in this age of crisis, when errors in thinking threatened the Christian gospel. His recent works *Original Sin* and *Freedom of the Will* had contributed to the spiritual warfare against infidelity, but he had a more ambitious plan: to write "a body of divinity in an entire new method," structuring all of "Christian theology" in a historical narrative. He would title this work *A History of the Work of Redemption,* and it would be based on a series of sermons Edwards delivered on that topic in 1739. Such a major work would certainly be difficult to complete with all the responsibilities of a college president.

And yet, surprisingly, after listing all his faults that made him unfit for the job and detailing the scholarly plans that made the job unfit for him, Edwards did not decline the offer. And after much discussion and deliberation, he accepted the presidency of the College of New Jersey, and he left for Princeton in 1758. Sarah and the children planned to join him in a few months, after he was settled.[1]

Soon after arriving in New Jersey, Edwards acted on his typical faith in modern science by receiving an inoculation for smallpox—a new, risky, and controversial treatment at the time. (More reliable vaccines, as opposed to dangerous inoculations, would not be discovered until the end of the century.) Tragically, Jonathan Edwards contracted smallpox from this inoculation and died on March 22, 1758. Sarah and most of the family had not yet joined Jonathan, but he did not die alone. His daughters Esther and Lucy were in Princeton, and on his deathbed he dictated the following message to Lucy: "Give my kindest love to my dear wife, and tell her, that the uncommon union, which has so long subsisted between us, has been of such a nature, as I trust is spiritual, and therefore will continue forever: and I hope she will be supported under so great a trial, and

149

submit cheerfully to the will of God."[2] These last words to his wife reflected the divine, spiritual love that he found central to all reality—a love that embraces the will of God and exudes joy even in the most severe trials.

Jonathan Edwards's passing marked the beginning of a legacy that rivals that of any religious figure in American history. We often look to the eighteenth century to recall the "founding fathers" of the United States—the Washingtons, Jeffersons, and Franklins. In a very similar way, Edwards was a founding father of American religious experience. To examine Edwards's vast influence in full detail would require books, not short chapters. But in a few pages we can gain an appreciation of Edwards's legacy in three important scenes that represent the breadth of his presence in American religious life.

A Legacy Begun

Scene One: American Slavery

Almost immediately after Edwards's death, through the nineteenth century, Jonathan Edwards's thought influenced the debate over American slavery. And it was most clearly seen in the life of his students, particularly Samuel Hopkins. Hopkins was a Connecticut-born, Yale-educated minister who devoted his life to learning from Edwards and developing his ideas in new directions. He practically lived with the Edwards family for much of his young life. He spent endless hours in conversations with his teacher in both Northampton and Stockbridge. When Edwards died, the family left his valuable and unpublished manuscripts in Hopkins's care. Not only did Hopkins become the guardian of Edwards's papers, but he also saw himself as a guardian of the tradition that Edwards represented. This was an important task for Hopkins and other students of Edwards, especially Joseph Bellamy, and Edwards's son, Jonathan Edwards Jr. Together, they formed a school of thought around Edwards's theology. However, while they greatly admired Edwards, they adapted his ideas in ways that Edwards had not imagined. Their creativity with traditional Calvinism got them into trouble with some Calvinists, who labeled them "New Divinity" men. And by "new" they certainly did not mean "improved."

While the New Divinity theologians preached, taught, and wrote, the slave trade escalated in America, and perceptive observers realized that slavery was the great moral evil in American history. But for all his insight into human depravity, Edwards had been blind to the injustice of slavery; on this issue Edwards was a man of his times, a believer in a society built on traditional hierarchies and deference to superiors. Samuel Hopkins looked beyond his teacher's limited worldview and perceived slavery in all its gross injustice. But it was Edwards's ideas of Christian virtue that made him see slavery so clearly.

Hopkins spent much of his ministry in a Congregational church in Newport, Rhode Island, where he witnessed firsthand the evils of slavery. The inhuman treatment of slaves appalled him, and he despised the greed that justified the grossly unjust trafficking of human life. Even more appalling for Hopkins were the Christian defenses of slavery. A disturbing number of Christians considered slavery a biblically approved way of doing business. The Bible said a lot about slavery, they claimed, and most often biblical writers either assumed the justness of slavery or at least refused to condemn it. In opposition, Hopkins drew on Edwards's notion of Christian virtue—that it was a love of God above all other loyalties, one that empowered a corresponding love of all God's creation. Edwards defined this concept of true virtue as "benevolence to being in general," and while Hopkins appreciated Edwards's intention,

he thought his definition was too abstract. Hopkins worried that if he wrote about "benevolence to being in general" his readers would be confused and not be motivated to virtuous action. So Hopkins adapted Edwards's idea of true virtue and stated it more forcefully as "disinterested benevolence." By "disinterested benevolence" Hopkins meant a goodness or love that is unbiased by selfish interests. This kind of "disinterested" love would focus on the needs of the lowest and weakest in society—namely, African slaves. He hoped that this "disinterested benevolence" would replace the self-centered and ruthless capitalism so foundational to the slave trade.

In 1776—the year that symbolizes American liberty—Hopkins issued a call to end the slave trade addressed directly to the representatives of the thirteen colonies. *A Dialogue Concerning the Slavery of the Africans* was published before the Declaration of Independence, but Hopkins knew the liberating tone of the era. In the *Dialogue*, he argued that slavery violated the "whole tenor of divine revelation," just as it clashed with the liberating spirit of 1776. In churches, homes, and street corners, patriotic colonists discussed the need to liberate themselves from the "slavery" of their British oppressors. And yet these same patriots did not care that their slaves overheard this talk of liberty from masters who kept them in bondage. What a gross inconsistency! How amazing that freedom-loving colonists held slaves, "tyrannizing" the "poor blacks who have as good a claim to liberty" as any white patriot.[3]

In Samuel Hopkins, therefore, Edwards's legacy was not merely intellectual; it was practical, an explicit call to transform society. Tragically, the new nation did not immediately heed Hopkins's word, but his arguments and the Edwardsian ideas that formed their foundation would be heard from again in the battle against slavery. Shortly

before the Civil War we can locate Edwards's influence on John Brown, the radical abolitionist who led several violent strikes against slaveholders, culminating in his attack on the armory at Harpers Ferry, Virginia, in 1859. Brown's family came from Puritan stock, and he was an avid reader of Edwards's sermons. In his violent revolts against slavery, he drew from Edwards's "Sinners in the Hands of an Angry God," applying Edwards's hellfire threats to slaveholders, charging that they would soon feel God's vengeance for their evil commerce in human life.[4] Today most people recognize Brown from the song they sing in his honor, "John Brown's Body," which became the basis for Julia Ward Howe's "Battle Hymn of the Republic." Brown was hardly a typical abolitionist—but he was a great admirer of Edwards, and, in truth, that admiration fueled his violent attacks on slavery. Brown was an extreme case, but an apt case of one who drew from

Edwards and focused his religious sense of justice into efforts to change American society.

Thus in both Samuel Hopkins and John Brown we can identify Edwards's legacy in reforms leading to the abolition of slavery. Most often, however, Edwards's influence in American social reform came through his most visible religious legacy: the dramatic episodes of revivals throughout American history.

Scene Two: The American Revivals

In 1949, in the midst of his first crusade in Los Angeles, the famous American evangelist Billy Graham did something unusual—he preached a two-hundred-year-old sermon. The message that Graham chose for the L.A. multitudes was none other than Jonathan Edwards's "Sinners in the Hands of an Angry God." Graham introduced the sermon with a tribute to Edwards, proclaiming to the crowd that "Jonathan Edwards was one of the greatest scholars that America ever produced, one of the greatest preachers, a man of tremendous conviction, a man that we look back on today and revere, and pray that God might raise up again such men on the American scene, that will not compromise, but will preach the word of God seriously."[5] As Graham's tribute to Edwards demonstrates, Americans will always identify Edwards with revival, and rightly so. But Graham's introduction of Edwards makes it clear that he chose Edwards's sermon not only because he thought that the sin city of Los Angeles needed a taste of hellfire preaching (though that was surely one of Graham's goals). Instead, Graham emphasized Edwards's scholarly credentials. Edwards combined intellectual credibility and heartfelt revival preaching. To Graham, Edwards was an authority on revivals that modern-day preachers needed to remember and to imitate, just as Billy Graham did in that Los Angeles crusade.

It was only natural that Graham looked to Edwards as an authority on revivals. When it comes to revivals, Edwards is one of America's most prestigious authorities. While he and Whitefield led the way in stirring revivals to life in colonial America, Edwards was the primary intellectual force behind them. He not only described the revivals with scientific precision, he also articulated the best theological analysis of revivals and their implications for Christianity around the world. And because revivals have been almost constant in its history, this work is profoundly important for our understanding of America.

From Edwards to Graham and beyond, revivals have reshaped Christianity in the United States. Under the influence of revival, people have founded new denominations

and breathed new life into existing traditions. Revivals have launched hundreds of efforts to reform society in various ways, from defeating slavery to combating poverty. Most visibly, revivals are largely responsible for the emergence and continued strength of evangelicalism in the United States in all its teeming diversity—from Baptists and Methodists to Pentecostals and the various nondenominational groups. Revivals have been and continue to be occasions of redemption from sin and healing from illness. Revivals have also launched the careers of religious celebrities and helped to create a culture of televangelism and religious marketing. While Edwards did not underestimate the power of revival, even he could not have imagined the ways in which revival would shape the American religious landscape.

The transformative influence of revival that started with Edwards and Whitefield surged again in a cluster of revivals that began about fifty years after Edwards's death. We refer to these revivals as the Second Great Awakening—a name that signifies their continuity with the revivals that Edwards and Whitefield made famous. Compared to the First Great Awakening, the Second Great Awakening was broader, bolder, more emotionally frantic, and perhaps even more conflicted. Keeping track of this period's theological divisions and quarrels could frustrate the most patient saint (or scholar, in this case). Theologians argued over the revivals and other issues and eventually divided into various groups with an array of labels, including one we have already noted, "New Divinity," in addition to "Old Calvinism," and "New Haven Theology"—and these were just a few. Even in the midst of this teeming diversity in revival scope, theology, and practice, Edwards's presence loomed large as the founder of American revivalism and the esteemed expert whose guidance could perhaps be a beacon in the conflicts of early evangelicalism.

At first glance it may seem surprising that Edwards was relevant at all in the Second Great Awakening; these revivals were vastly different from those that Edwards knew. Regionally, the Second Great Awakening covered much more ground than the earlier revivals, including not only New England and the middle states but the South and the old Southwest as well. Theologically, the First Great Awakening was overall a much more Calvinist affair. Calvinism was certainly alive and well in the Second Great Awakening, especially in the Northeast. Even so, Edwards would have been horrified to see many later revivalists reject his sacred Calvinism in strong terms. The Arminian revivalists tended to reject original sin and human depravity outright, while bashing predestination and election as outrageous, irrational insults. While Edwards had believed Arminianism to be the greatest threat to revival, Methodist revivalists a century later thought the same way about Calvinism. Even so, Edwards's influence was profound in nearly all phases of the Second Great Awakening.

Edwards's reach into this period is easiest to see in the New England phase of the new revivals.[6] In part, it was a family matter. Edwards's grandson Timothy Dwight, president of Yale, sounded what many believe to be the opening bell of the Second Great Awakening by preaching to his students against the evils of enlightened deism and radical French thought. One of the students converted under Dwight's preaching was the influential revivalist and social reformer Lyman Beecher. Incidentally, Beecher's first revival preaching began with a sermon against dueling, precipitated by the 1804 duel between Vice President Aaron Burr Jr. and Alexander Hamilton. As it turned out, Burr won the duel, fatally wounding Hamilton, but Burr's reputation never recovered, and his famous act of violence inadvertently

launched a revival. What an incredible irony, given that Aaron Burr was Jonathan Edwards's grandson!

Dueling sermons aside, Lyman Beecher was a preacher and theologian who shaped his theology to new agendas in the new nation. In a postrevolutionary age, when people craved freedom as both citizens and Christians, Beecher accepted the fact that church establishments were on the way out. The First Amendment prevented Congress from establishing a national church, and the days of established churches in individual states were numbered. But the government did not need to support religion, Beecher came to believe. An even stronger force was revival. Revival inspired people to action, and Beecher found that not only could revivals motivate individual salvation. They could also motivate social action, specifically the moral reform of society.

As many have surmised, Lyman Beecher's powerful

preaching and sensitivity to reform affected his children deeply. To be sure, he is perhaps best known as the father of renowned minister and theologian Henry Ward Beecher and famous novelist Harriet Beecher Stowe. Stowe's unforgettable novel, *Uncle Tom's Cabin*, heavily influenced abolitionist zeal and contributed to much regional division over slavery. Some even claim that Stowe's novel made war inevitable. Though Stowe had no love for Edwards's theology, even once calling it a "poetry of torture," she recognized the value of Edwards's theological tradition in the antislavery convictions of Samuel Hopkins. In fact, in one of Stowe's novels, *The Minister's Wooing*, she cast Hopkins in a heroic role—as a religious reformer who fought courageously for the freedom of slaves, despite his distasteful Calvinist doctrines.

Like Lyman Beecher, Nathaniel William Taylor was a student of Timothy Dwight at Yale, and he worked to make Calvinism less distasteful to some of its critics. Taylor was a

New Haven pastor turned professor, who later became the Dwight Professor of Didactic Theology at Yale. Though Taylor committed himself to the theological tradition of Edwards, he adapted his ideas to speak to the needs of revival in his day. Worried that the traditional view of original sin would harm revival success in this new nation built on democracy and independence, Taylor emphasized that sin is an issue of action, not an inherited trait that we can do nothing about. Taylor believed Edwards was correct in his view that we are all depraved sinners, but he respectfully differed with Edwards's explanation for depravity. We are sinners because we sin, Taylor agued. We damage our own souls with our own actions, and we can blame only ourselves. Like Beecher, Taylor embraced a revival theology that fit the modern times—a free gospel call to a free people.

Outside of the New England arena of the Second Great Awakening, Edwards's presence is a bit more surprising, and yet it was just as influential. Edwards spent much of his life and writings in revival controversies, and he remained mired in disputes over revival nearly a century after his death. And Edwards was not only involved in revival controversies; he always seemed to be caught in the middle of any number of intellectual disputes. Even in the century after he died he was once again in the middle of a revival debate, this time centered on Charles Finney, a lawyer turned preacher, whose revivals flourished in such cities as New York, Philadelphia, and Rochester.

Though Charles Finney's success was undeniable, his methods were highly questionable. Revivals, in Finney's view, were not miracles mysteriously delivered from God. No, revivals were not mystery but *science*. If one applies the proper techniques, revivals will result at the time and place of one's choosing. While Finney called these techniques "new measures," critics condemned them and accused

Finney of doing more harm than good by perverting God's true means of rescuing sinners. And in the debates between Finney and his critics, both sides claimed to be the faithful heirs of Jonathan Edwards. Finney's opponents viewed Edwards as the humble intellectual who protected the integrity of revival by rejecting the haughty and overzealous fanatics who disrupted the order of churches and lampooned the authority of respectable ministers. But Finney would not be outdone. He claimed Edwards for his side, arguing that Edwards was not afraid to adopt "new measures" of his own. In Finney's view, Edwards was the daring innovator who rebuked stodgy rationalists for dismissing revival just because some converts let their emotions get the best of them. Edwards was not afraid to buck tradition, as when he bravely rejected his grandfather Stoddard's practice of offering Communion to everyone, regardless of a testimony of faith. This was the ultimate "new measure,"

in Finney's view, one for which Edwards was willing to lose his pastorate. These connections that Finney tried to draw between himself and Edwards were questionable, and Finney's opponents questioned them at every point. Even so, Finney's need to call on Edwards's authority indicates Edwards's importance as a founding father of American revivalism. Later revivalists could indeed disagree with Edwards's theology, but they had to be respectful in their disagreements and bow humbly to Edwards's legacy.

In Finney's day and beyond, some evangelicals took revivals to an emotional level that would have shocked Edwards. The great camp meeting revival at Cane Ridge, Kentucky, in 1801 was just the largest example of a new form of revival on the frontier. These camp meeting revivals could last for weeks at a time and involve thousands of people from various denominations. And these were hardly quiet, reverent affairs. Preachers often worked themselves into a fevered pitch as their congregations responded with emotional fits. Under the influence of camp meeting preaching, some people fell down in agony while others jerked uncontrollably as the spirit moved. Some even danced, including a few Baptists. Not all Baptists and Methodists went to camp meetings, but even in their local congregations they experienced revivals regularly. And the results were dramatic. Empowered by revivals, Methodists and Baptists became the fastest-growing Protestant denominations in the nineteenth century.

These evangelical revivals were much different from those of Edwards and Whitefield. Not only was the emotionalism turned up to a higher degree, but also the theology was different. It would have pained Edwards to know that future revivalists in America would reject much of his Calvinist theology. Still, even Arminian Methodists admired Edwards as a model preacher and revival expert.

Evangelicals reprinted Edwards's *Faithful Narrative* and used it as a prototype of the popular revival narrative that multiplied in the nineteenth century. *Religious Affections* also became a classic evangelical text, constantly reprinted, though always carefully edited to remove Calvinist dangers. Methodists, for instance, could read an edition of *Religious Affections* edited by John Wesley himself. Wesley admired *Religious Affections*, but noted that its nourishment for the spirit was unfortunately tainted with strains of poisonous Calvinism. Theological tolerance could only go so far, even for the sake of revival.

In addition, Methodists and other evangelicals embraced the practical, spiritual wisdom of Edwards's writings on personal reflection, including his *Personal Narrative* and his "Resolutions." Several denominational

publishers and tract societies reprinted these works for spiritual edification. Inspired by these writings, evangelicals praised Edwards's humility, his longing for true religious experience, and above all, his absolute dedication to living life for God at every moment. Not only Arminian Methodists but also moderate Calvinist Baptists in the South admired the pietistic Edwards. For example, Basil Manly Jr., a hymn writer and professor at Southern Baptist Theological Seminary, saw Edwards as a model for spiritual life. In comparison with Edwards, Manly chastised himself for his cold, languishing piety, and, imitating Edwards, he developed his own catalog of resolutions to deepen his spiritual discipline.

Perhaps Jonathan Edwards's most enduring spiritual legacy was his *Life of David Brainerd*—his best selling book in the nineteenth century, both in America and in Britain. In *Life of David Brainerd*, Edwards published his theology in the form of a life story—a biography of redemption and piety, a life that represented an affectionate dedication to God. Edwards's edition of Brainerd's diary depicted him as missionary hero, a model of affectionate religion, and a self-sacrificial, godly life. And the result was a Christian classic that influenced countless evangelicals to devote their lives to missions and social reform. John Wesley was enthralled with Edwards's *Brainerd*. He urged Methodists to look for "preachers of David Brainerd's spirit," for they could withstand all adversity in service to the gospel. Later, Wesley edited and published several editions of *Brainerd* himself, and advised that all preachers "be followers of him, as he was of Christ, in absolute self-devotion, in total deadness to the world." Edwards could not have been more pleased with such praise—even from an Arminian.[7]

Edwards, therefore, influenced later evangelicals in at

least three ways. In their revival practice they hailed Edwards's legendary accomplishments and his scientific analysis of the effects of revival success. In their personal piety they found in Edwards a model of humility and entire devotion to God—despite his theological devotion to Calvinism. And in the *Life of David Brainerd*, evangelicals embraced a narrative description of Edwards's theology that fit perfectly with their zeal for missions.

Scene Three: American History, Neo-Orthodoxy, and the University

How should we understand Edwards's significance in American history? In the early twentieth century, several historians were unimpressed with Edwards's legacy for America. Consider historian Vernon L. Parrington's treatment of Edwards in his important book, *Main Currents in American Thought*; the title of one of his chapters is revealing: "The Anachronism of Jonathan Edwards." Edwards, according to Parrington, was tragically brilliant—he had a great mind, but wasted it on an outdated Calvinist theology. The wave of the future was enlightened liberalism and democracy, which was the direct opposite of the authoritarian and terrifying theology of Edwards. In one telling phrase, he called Edwards's *Freedom of the Will* "the last great defense of the conservatism that was stifling the intellectual life of New England." The great "tragedy" of Edwards's life was that of a wasted intellect. In Edwards's mind, "the theologian triumphed over the philosopher." In the end, Edwards devoted "his noble gifts to the thankless task of re-imprisoning the mind" rather than liberating it. Edwards "was called to be a transcendental emancipator, but he remained a Calvinist." And as a gloomy Calvinist, Parrington concluded, Edwards had no guidance for a

modern American nation that looked toward an optimistic future of advancement.[8]

Parrington would not have the last word. Shortly after his *Main Currents* was published in 1927 his hopes for a triumphal liberalism in America were dashed in the stock market crash of 1929 and the economic depression that plagued the 1930s. To make matters worse, a second world war loomed at the end of the decade. During this period, the optimistic, liberal theology that put all confidence in technological advancement and human goodness met strong challenges from a movement known as neo-orthodoxy. Theologians representing neo-orthodoxy, led by Swiss thinker Karl Barth, asserted that the modern world could learn a lot from premodern theologies that many had believed were hopelessly out of date. Suddenly, Edwards's Calvinist beliefs in the pervasiveness of sin and a sovereign God seemed to reflect the realties of the twentieth century. American leaders in the neo-orthodox movement were brothers Reinhold Niebuhr and H. Richard Niebuhr. Both had formerly been liberals and both gained a new appreciation of Edwards in ominous modern times. In his book entitled *The Kingdom of God in America*, H. Richard Niebuhr wrote that America needed Edwards's vision of a sovereign God. The problem was that liberal theology preached that "a God without wrath brought [humans] without sin into a kingdom without judgment through the ministrations of a Christ without a cross." In Niebuhr's view, America needed to recapture the prophetic role of religion that Edwards preached about, a vision of God's judgment that could call the world's values into question and offer redemption for a threatened humanity.[9]

Shortly after World War II, this new appreciation for Edwards's legacy reached its height in a biography of Edwards published by Harvard professor Perry Miller. Anyone today who thinks the Puritans are interesting probably owes something to Perry Miller. He was the scholar most responsible for the modern appreciation of Puritanism. Though Miller was more atheist than Calvinist in his theology, he appreciated the Puritans for their heroic efforts to understand an unknowable God. And like the neo-orthodox theologians, Miller sympathized with Calvinist views of depravity, judgment, and the necessity of a prophetic voice for American culture. When Miller read Jonathan Edwards, he believed he had found the height of the heroic, Puritan intellect. And yet Miller's description of Edwards seemed far too modern. "The truth is," Miller claimed, "Edwards was infinitely more than a theologian. He was one of America's five or six major artists, who happened to work with ideas instead of with poems or novels." Further, Miller's Edwards "speaks from an insight into science and psychology so much ahead of his time that our own can hardly be said to have caught up with him."[10] Miller saw Edwards wrestling with modern problems that would persist into the twentieth century, problems that neo-orthodox theologians would later come to terms with much as Edwards did. It's no wonder that Reinhold Niebuhr called Miller's book "a brilliant biographical study."[11]

The Current Scene: Academic Respectability and Evangelical Credibility

While some called Perry Miller's biography of Edwards brilliant and others called it brilliantly wrong, all agreed that Miller started a lasting conversation about Edwards's significance for America. Of equal importance, Miller recognized the need for a modern, academic edition of Edwards's writings, and he led the way in launching the Yale edition of *The Works of Jonathan Edwards*. The first volume, *Freedom of the Will*, came off the press in 1957. Fifty years later the twenty-sixth and final volume is complete. Working under the direction of the Jonathan Edwards Center at Yale University, scholars have combed through Edwards's vast writings, deciphering his almost illegible handwriting to transcribe his sermons, and preparing his many notebooks and letters for publication. The Yale edition of Edwards' writings has been the catalyst for the ever-increasing scholarly interest in Edwards—much of which has corrected Miller's overzealous claims for Edwards's modernity, seeking instead to understand Edwards in his own time and place.

Recent scholars agree with Miller that Edwards was a dazzling intellect, but they find his brilliance in his theological worldview, closely tied to his predecessors in the Puritan tradition and his heirs in modern evangelicalism. So in contrast to Miller, many of today's scholars conclude that Edwards was not only among the first modern intellectuals; he was also among the first American evangelicals, and was perhaps America's greatest theologian. This was the perspective of George Marsden's authoritative biography, *Jonathan Edwards: A Life*, published in 2003. Marsden asserted that Edwards was not an evangelical in the modern sense—he lived in a different world, socially, politically, and intellectually. Still, Edwards was a pivotal influence on the evangelical traditions that flourished after the Revolution. Imagine what the United States would be like without the influence of evangelicals from the nineteenth century to today. The nation would be dramatically different socially, politically, and religiously. Compared with other modern nations, the United States is much more "religious," not only in the civil religion that pervades the national identity, but also in the number of citizens who frequently attend religious services. Why? Certainly the success of evangelicalism is a central explanation. And why was evangelicalism so successful? Certainly it had a lot to do with the uncontainable flourishing, in many times and places, of Edwards's beloved revivalism. So when historians describe how modern America came to be what it is today, the story of Edwards deserves special attention, alongside founders of the United States such as Benjamin Franklin. Not that Edwards's story is relevant only to American history. To be sure, Edwards has a place in international histories of Christianity. Revivals were international realities in Edwards's day, a fact that he celebrated and worked to support, just as revivals today expand beyond national, not to mention denominational, borders. Understandably, then, the scholarship on Edwards is multifaceted, engaging historians, theologians, philosophers, ethicists, and various other scholars. Three hundred years after his birth Edwards has a well-deserved place in the university.[12]

But Edwards doesn't fascinate only scholars. More and more pastors are teaching their congregations about Edwards, and he has even captured the attention of young evangelicals. The media have taken notice. A 2006 cover of *Christianity Today* featured a young man sporting a T-shirt with an image of Edwards on the front, surrounded by the slogan "Jonathan Edwards Is My Homeboy." The article, titled "Young, Restless, and Reformed," describes the resurgence of Calvinist theology in a variety of evangelical churches, colleges, and seminaries, including Trinity Evangelical Divinity School and the Southern Baptist Theological Seminary. Edwards has been pivotal to this reawakening of Calvinism. Consider the example of Baptist minister and author John Piper, whose popular books include the 1998 bestseller *God's Passion for His Glory: Living the Vision of Jonathan Edwards*. And which of Edwards's writings does Piper highlight in this book? We might expect a few of Edwards's revival sermons perhaps, or maybe a selection from *Religious Affections?* Surprisingly, Piper's book features a complete reprinting of one of Edwards's most complicated theological and philosophical works: *The End for Which God Created the World*. In this profound but densely argued treatise, Piper finds a great example of what he calls "Christian Hedonism," the pleasure the Christian finds in glorifying God above all. It's amazing that a work that Edwards crafted in response to the moral philosophy of the Enlightenment has found such a popular application in evangelical circles today. But, as Piper pointed out, Edwards's theological and philosophical expertise is vital for today's church. Included in Piper's book are sections entitled "A Personal Encounter with Jonathan Edwards" and "How Would Edwards Use the Internet?" In these discussions, Edwards is important because he combined intellectual rigor with heartfelt devotion. Piper even wrote that "Edwards had ushered me closer into the presence of God than any other writer has." In the minds of many, therefore, Edwards has become the evangelicals' model academic—one who combined rigorous scholarship with fervent piety.[13]

These brief scenes reveal only glimpses of Edwards's legacies. There is much more to appreciate, many more

appearances of Edwards in American history that span far beyond the mere "images and shadows" that I have sketched in this chapter. But even these partial glances reveal several major dimensions of Edwards's influence. As revivalist, theologian, and philosopher, he inspired abolitionists, novelists, ethicists, and all kinds of preachers, including modern evangelists. He became the paradigmatic colonial intellectual and a perennial model for evangelicalism. He became a prophetic voice for twentieth-century reappraisals of the American spirit, and consequently he became a topic of study in a variety of academic departments. Certainly Edwards's image as a hellfire preacher remains, though it hardly has the last word. Edwards will always reward those who read deeper in his works, keeping in mind the "lively affections" that empowered his ideas.

Notes

Introduction

1. *WJE* 22:411. *WJE* refers herein to *The Works of Jonathan Edwards*, general editors Perry Miller, John Smith, and Harry Stout, 26 vols. (New Haven: Yale University Press, 1957–2008).

1. The Young Edwards

1. George Marsden, *Jonathan Edwards: A Life* (New Haven: Yale University Press, 2003), 19.
2. *WJE* 16:791.
3. Ibid.
4. Marsden, *Jonathan Edwards*, 26–28.
5. See Harry S. Stout, *The New England Soul: Preaching and Religious Culture in Colonial New England* (New York: Oxford University Press, 1986).
6. Marsden, *Jonathan Edwards*, 37–39.
7. *WJE* 2:165. Cited in Marsden, *Jonathan Edwards*, 48.
8. *WJE* 16:789.
9. Marsden, *Jonathan Edwards*, 52.
10. *WJE* 16:742–43, 753, 756.
11. Marsden, *Jonathan Edwards*, 64–66.
12. *WJE* 6:163–69. "The Spider Letter" is also printed in *A Jonathan Edwards Reader* ed. John Smith, Harry Stout, and Kenneth Minkema (New Haven: Yale University Press, 1995), 1–8.
13. See *WJE* 11:4–6.
14. *WJE* 11:191.
15. *WJE* 11:34–38.

16. See Marsden, *Jonathan Edwards*, 73–74.
17. *WJE* 11:59, 70, 75–76, 106.
18. Marsden, *Jonathan Edwards*, 66–67.
19. See David Hall, *Worlds of Wonder, Days of Judgment: Popular Religious Belief in Early New England* (Cambridge, MA: Harvard University Press, 1990).
20. Marsden, *Jonathan Edwards*, 68–71.
21. *WJE* 6:241; cf. Stephen Daniel, "Edwards as Philosopher," in *The Cambridge Companion to Jonathan Edwards*, ed. Stephen Stein (Cambridge: Cambridge University Press, 2007), 168.
22. See Norman Fiering, *Jonathan Edwards's Moral Thought and Its British Context* (Chapel Hill: University of North Carolina Press, 1981), 200–260, esp. 207–13.
23. *WJE* 16:792–94. See also E. Brooks Holifield, *Theology in America: Christian Thought from the Age of the Puritans to the Civil War* (New Haven: Yale University Press, 2003), 104–5; and *WJE* 8:332–93.
24. *WJE* 16:789–90, 792–96.
25. Jonathan Edwards, "A Divine and Supernatural Light," in *The Sermons of Jonathan Edwards: A Reader*, ed. Wilson Kimnach, Kenneth Minkema, and Douglas Sweeney (New Haven: Yale University Press, 1999), 126–27. Marsden, *Jonathan Edwards*, 96
26. *WJE* 16:797. See also, *WJE* 14:75.

2. An Affection for Revival

1. Harry Stout, "Edwards as Revivalist," in *The Cambridge Companion to Jonathan Edwards*, ed. Stephen Stein (Cambridge: Cambridge University Press, 2007), 140.
2. *WJE* 22:411–12.
3. *WJE* 22:410–12.
4. *WJE* 4:97–211.
5. George Marsden, *Jonathan Edwards: A Life* (New Haven: Yale University Press, 2003), 73.
6. *WJE* 4:146, 150, 158–59.
7. *WJE* 4:194–207.
8. Harry Stout, *The Divine Dramatist: George Whitefield and the*

Rise of Modern Evangelism (Grand Rapids: Wm. B. Eerdmans, 1991).

9. Richard L. Bushman, ed., *The Great Awakening: Documents on the Revival of Religion, 1740–1745* (Chapel Hill: University of North Carolina Press), 21, 45–55.

10. Charles Goen, "Introduction," *WJE* 4:52–53; see also *WJE* 4:213–88.

11. *WJE* 2:84.

12. *WJE* 2:95–99.

13. *WJE* 2:120.

14. *WJE* 2:127–35.

15. *WJE* 2:193–461.

16. *WJE* 2:191–208.

17. *WJE* 2:383–411.

3. Exodus from Northampton

1. George Marsden, *Jonathan Edwards: A Life* (New Haven: Yale University Press, 2003), 230. Much of the biographical information in this chapter draws on Marsden's narrative, unless otherwise noted.

2. See Jonathan Edwards, "The Bad Book Case," in *A Jonathan Edwards Reader*, ed. John Smith, Harry Stout, and Kenneth Minkema (New Haven: Yale University Press, 1995), 173.

3. Ibid., 175–78. See also Marsden, *Jonathan Edwards*, 298–99.

4. For an explanation of Puritan convictions regarding purity and power, see Harry S. Stout, *The New England Soul: Preaching and Religious Culture in Colonial New England* (New York: Oxford University Press, 1986), 14–15, passim.

5. See Edmund Morgan, *Visible Saints: The History of a Puritan Idea* (New York: New York University Press, 1963), 113–38.

6. Marsden, *Jonathan Edwards*, 341–74.

4. Freedom of the Will?

1. Alexander Pope, "Essay on Man," in *The Poetical Works of Alexander Pope* (Frederick Warne, 1866), 76.

2. Paul Ramsey, "Editors Introduction," *WJE* 1:3.

3. Allen Guelzo, "Freedom of the Will," in *The Princeton Companion to Jonathan Edwards*, ed. Sang Hyun Lee (Princeton, NJ: Princeton University Press, 2005), 118.
4. George Marsden, *Jonathan Edwards: A Life* (New Haven: Yale University Press, 2003), 140.
5. Jonathan Edwards, *The Sermons of Jonathan Edwards: A Reader*, ed. Wilson Kimnach, Kenneth Minkema, and Douglas Sweeney (New Haven: Yale University Press, 1999), 67, 80.
6. See Ramsey, "Editors Introduction," *WJE* 1:66–67, 82, 90.
7. Kenneth Minkema, e-mail correspondence, 8/3/2007.
8. *WJE* 1:141–44. See also an edited version, Jonathan Edwards, "Freedom of the Will," in *A Jonathan Edwards Reader*, ed. John Smith, Harry Stout, and Kenneth Minkema (New Haven: Yale University Press, 1995), 196.
9. *WJE* 6:376. Cited in Ramsey, "Editors Introduction," *WJE* 1:57.
10. *WJE* 1:156–62.
11. *WJE* 1:362–63.
12. See Paul Ramsey's discussion, "Editors Introduction," *WJE* 1:37–38.
13. *WJE* 1:163–65.
14. Isaac Watts, *Essay on the Freedom of the Will*, quoted by Edwards in *WJE* 1:195.
15. *WJE* 1:172–83.
16. *WJE* 1:304, 326, 357.

5. Original Sin

1. *WJE* 3:435. See also an edited version, Jonathan Edwards, "The Great Christian Doctrine of Original Sin Defended," in *A Jonathan Edwards Reader*, ed. John Smith, Harry Stout, and Kenneth Minkema (New Haven: Yale University Press, 1995), 223–43.
2. *WJE* 12:502.
3. *WJE* 3:3.
4. *WJE* 3:102.
5. *WJE* 12:499–502.

6. *WJE* 3:348.
7. *WJE* 3:107.
8. *WJE* 3:120, 160–61.
9. *WJE* 3:120–33.
10. *WJE* 3:193.
11. *WJE* 3:380–83.
12. *WJE* 3:380–403; *WJE* 22:411–12. See also Edwards, "Sinners in the Hands of an Angry God," in *Jonathan Edwards Reader*, 97–98.
13. *WJE* 3:142.

6. Creation and True Virtue

1. *WJE* 16:696; Paul Ramsey, "Editors Introduction," in *WJE* 8:5.
2. *WJE* 16:421.
3. *WJE* 16:429.
4. *WJE* 16:430–31.
5. *WJE* 16:433.
6. *WJE* 16:442.
7. Ibid.
8. *WJE* 16:443.
9. *WJE* 16:444.
10. *WJE* 16:459.
11. James Hutson, *The Founders on Religion: A Book of Quotations* (Princeton, NJ: Princeton University Press, 2003), 147; George Marsden, *Jonathan Edwards: A Life* (New Haven: Yale University Press, 2003), 464–68.
12. *WJE* 16:552.
13. *WJE* 16:539.
14. Ibid.
15. *WJE* 16:540.
16. *WJE* 16:541.
17. *WJE* 16:550.
18. Ibid.
19. *WJE* 16:551.
20. *WJE* 16:554–55.
21. *WJE* 16:552.

22. *WJE* 16:557.
23. *WJE* 16:559.
24. *WJE* 16:589–90.
25. *WJE* 16:597.
26. *WJE* 16:598–99.
27. *WJE* 16:609–11.

7. A Legacy Begun

1. *WJE* 16:725–30.
2. Quoted in S.E. Dwight's memoir in *The Works of President Edwards, with a Memoir of his Life*, ed. S. E. Dwight (New York: S. Converse, 1829), 1:578. Cf. also George Marsden, *Jonathan Edwards: A Life* (New Haven: Yale University Press, 2003), 494.
3. Samuel Hopkins, *The Works of Samuel Hopkins*, vol. 2, *A Dialogue Concerning the Slavery of the Africans* (Boston: Doctrinal Tract and Book Society, 1852), 562, 570–71, 585.
4. David Reynolds, *John Brown, Abolitionist: The Man Who Killed Slavery, Sparked the Civil War, and Seeded Civil Rights* (New York: Vintage, 2006), 151–52.
5. "Billy Graham & Sinners in the Hands of an Angry God," A Digital Exhibit from the Jonathan Edwards Center, Yale University, http://edwards.yale.edu/graham/.
6. The following discussion relies on Joseph Conforti, *Jonathan Edwards, Religious Tradition, and American Culture* (Chapel Hill: University of North Carolina Press, 1995), 11–68, 145–46.
7. *The Works of the Rev. John Wesley*, 14 vols., ed. Thomas Jackson (repr., Grand Rapids: Zondervan, 1960), 3:294, 8:328. Quoted in Conforti, *Jonathan Edwards*, 68.
8. See Vernon Parrington, *Main Currents in American Thought: An Interpretation of American Literature* (1927; New York: Harcourt, Brace, 1946), 157–63.
9. H. Richard Niebuhr, *The Kingdom of God in America*, with a new introduction by Martin Marty (Middletown, CT: Wesleyan University Press, 1988), 193.

10. Perry Miller, *Jonathan Edwards* (New York: William Sloane, 1949), xxxi–xxxii.

11. Reinhold Niebuhr, "Backwoods Genius," *The Nation* 169 (December 31, 1949), 648.

12. Marsden, *Jonathan Edwards*, 7–9; cf. Leigh E. Schmidt, "Review: The Edwards Revival: Or, the Public Consequences of Exceedingly Careful Scholarship," *The William and Mary Quarterly* 3rd ser. 58.2 (April 2001), 480–86.

13. Collin Hansen, "Young, Restless, and Reformed: Calvinism Is Making a Comeback—and Shaking Up the Church," *Christianity Today*, September 2006, 32–38. For John Piper's interpretation of Edwards, see Piper, *God's Passion for His Glory: Living the Vision of Jonathan Edwards* (Wheaton, IL: Crossway Books, 1998), and "Books That Have Influenced Me Most" and "We Want You to Be a Christian Hedonist!" http://www.desiringgod.org/.

For Further Reading

A main purpose of this book is to inspire readers to broaden their exploration of Edwards. The best starting point for researching Edwards is the Web site for the Jonathan Edwards Center at Yale University, http://edwards.yale.edu/. Led by director Harry S. Stout and executive director Kenneth P. Minkema, the Jonathan Edwards Center at Yale is the online extension of the authoritative printed edition of Edwards's writings, *The Works of Jonathan Edwards*, published by Yale University Press (see the first section that follows). The printed edition of the *Works* is complete in twenty-six volumes. But Edwards was so prolific that even these volumes represent slightly less than half of Edwards's total writings! The ambitious goal of the Jonathan Edwards Center is to expand beyond the printed editions to publish Edwards's complete works online, including his treatises, sermons, letters, and various notebooks. In addition, the Jonathan Edwards Center website is a fully featured source for research about Edwards on various levels, including teaching curricula, bibliographies, biographical material, and multimedia resources. The number of books and articles written about Edwards is staggering. An outstanding and recent guide to the massive research on Edwards is M. X. Lesser, *Reading Jonathan Edwards: An Annotated Bibliography in Three Parts, 1729–2005* (2007). Readers looking for an excellent biography should read *Jonathan Edwards: A Life,* by George M. Marsden—a comprehensive and engaging narrative of Edwards's life and thought. Also extraordinary for describing Edwards and his time is *The New England Soul: Preaching and Religious Culture in Colonial New England,* by Harry S. Stout. In the second section below, I have listed other exceptional studies. While this is not a definitive list, it should be enough to indicate the impressive breadth of Edwards scholarship.

Edwards' Works

The Works of Jonathan Edwards, general editors Perry Miller, John Smith, and Harry Stout, 26 vols. (New Haven: Yale University Press, 1957–2008).

1. *Freedom of the Will,* ed. Paul Ramsey (1957).
2. *Religious Affections,* ed. John Smith (1959).
3. *Original Sin,* ed. Clyde Holbrook (1970).
4. *The Great Awakening,* ed. C.C. Goen (1972).
5. *Apocalyptic Writings,* ed. Stephen Stein (1977).
6. *Scientific and Philosophical Writings,* ed. Wallace Anderson (1980).
7. *The Life of David Brainerd,* ed. Norman Pettit (1984).
8. *Ethical Writings,* ed. Paul Ramsey (1989).
9. *A History of the Work of Redemption,* ed. John Wilson (1989).
10. *Sermons and Discourses, 1720–1723,* ed. Wilson Kimnach (1992).
11. *Typological Writings,* ed. Wallace Anderson and David Watters (1993).
12. *Ecclesiastical Writings,* ed. David Hall (1994).
13. *The "Miscellanies," Entry Nos. a–z, aa–zz, 1–500,* ed. Thomas Schafer (1994).
14. *Sermons and Discourses, 1723–1729,* ed. Kenneth Minkema (1997).
15. *Notes on Scripture,* ed. Stephen Stein (1998).

16. *Letters and Personal Writings*, ed. George Claghorn (1998).
17. *Sermons and Discourses, 1730–1733*, ed. Mark Valeri (1999).
18. *The "Miscellanies," 501–832*, ed. Ava Chamberlain (2000).
19. *Sermons and Discourses, 1734–1738*, ed. M.X. Lesser (2001).
20. *The "Miscellanies," 833–1152*, ed. Amy Plantinga Pauw (2002).
21. *Writings on the Trinity, Grace, and Faith*, ed. Sang Hyun Lee (2002).
22. *Sermons and Discourses, 1739–1742*, ed. Harry Stout and Nathan Hatch, with Kyle Farley (2003).
23. *The "Miscellanies," 1153–1360*, ed. Douglas Sweeney (2004).
24. *The Blank Bible*, ed. Stephen Stein (2006).
25. *Sermons and Discourses, 1743–1758*, ed. Wilson Kimnach (2006).
26. *Catalogs of Reading*, ed. Peter J. Thuesen (2008).

Studies Concerning Edwards

Brown, Robert E. *Jonathan Edwards and the Bible.* Bloomington: Indiana University Press, 2002.

Chai, Leon. *Jonathan Edwards and the Limits of Enlightenment Philosophy.* New York: Oxford University Press, 1998.

Chamberlain, Ava. "Bad Books and Bad Boys: The Transformation of Gender in Eighteenth-Century Northampton, Massachusetts." *The New England Quarterly* 75, no. 2 (June 2002): 179–203.

———."The Immaculate Ovum: Jonathan Edwards and the Construction of the Female Body." *The William and Mary Quarterly* 3rd ser., 57, no. 2 (April 2000): 289–322.

Cherry, Conrad. *The Theology of Jonathan Edwards: A Reappraisal.* Bloomington: Indiana University Press, 1990.

For Further Reading

Conforti, Joseph A. *Jonathan Edwards, Religious Tradition & American Culture*. Chapel Hill: University of North Carolina Press, 1995.

———. *Samuel Hopkins and the New Divinity Movement: Calvinism, the Congregational Ministry, and Reform in New England between the Great Awakenings*. Grand Rapids: Wm. B. Eerdmans, 1981.

Crawford, Michael J. *Seasons of Grace: Colonial New England's Revival Tradition in Its British Context*. New York: Oxford University Press, 1991.

Danaher, William J. *The Trinitarian Ethics of Jonathan Edwards*. Louisville, KY: Westminster John Knox Press, 2004.

Daniel, Stephen H. *The Philosophy of Jonathan Edwards: A Study in Divine Semiotics*. Bloomington: Indiana University Press, 1994.

Delattre, Roland. "Aesthetics and Ethics: Jonathan Edwards and the Recovery of Aesthetics for Religious Ethics." *Journal of Religious Ethics* 31, no. 2 (2003): 277–97.

Edwards, Jonathan, *A Jonathan Edwards Reader*. Edited by John Edwin Smith, Harry S. Stout, and Kenneth P. Minkema. New Haven: Yale University Press, 1995.

Fiering, Norman Sanford. *Jonathan Edwards's Moral Thought and Its British Context*. Chapel Hill: University of North Carolina Press, 1981.

Gallagher, Edward. "'Sinners in the Hands of an Angry God': Some Unfinished Business." *The New England Quarterly* 73, no. 2 (June 2000): 202–21.

Gaustad, Edwin S. *The Great Awakening in New England*. New York: Harper & Bros., 1957.

Guelzo, Allen C. *Edwards on the Will: A Century of American Theological Debate*. Middletown, CT: Wesleyan University Press, 1989.

Gura, Philip F. *Jonathan Edwards: America's Evangelical*. New York: Hill & Wang, 2005.

Hall, David. "Jonathan Edwards in His Time, and in Ours." *Modern Intellectual History* 1, no. 3 (2004): 387–98.

Hall, David D. *Worlds of Wonder, Days of Judgment: Popular Reli-*

gious Belief in Early New England. Cambridge, MA: Harvard University Press, 1990.

Hatch, Nathan O., and Harry S. Stout. *Jonathan Edwards and the American Experience*. New York: Oxford University Press, 1988.

Holifield, E. Brooks. *The Covenant Sealed: The Development of Puritan Sacramental Theology in Old and New England, 1570–1720*. New Haven: Yale University Press, 1974.

———.*Theology in America: Christian Thought from the Age of the Puritans to the Civil War*. New Haven: Yale University Press, 2003.

Howe, Daniel Walker. *Making the American Self: Jonathan Edwards to Abraham Lincoln*. Cambridge, MA: Harvard University Press, 1997.

Jenson, Robert W. *America's Theologian: A Recommendation of Jonathan Edwards*. New York: Oxford University Press, 1988.

Johnson, Thomas H. "Jonathan Edwards and the 'Young Folks' Bible.'" *The New England Quarterly* 5, no. 1 (January 1932): 37–54.

Kidd, Thomas S. *The Great Awakening: The Roots of Evangelical Christianity in Colonial America*. New Haven: Yale University Press, 2007.

Kimnach, Wilson, Kenneth Minkema, and Douglas Sweeney, eds. *The Sermons of Jonathan Edwards: A Reader*. New Haven: Yale University Press, 1999.

Lee, Sang Hyun. *The Philosophical Theology of Jonathan Edwards*. Rev. and expanded ed. Princeton, NJ: Princeton University Press, 2000.

———, ed. *The Princeton Companion to Jonathan Edwards*. Princeton, N.J.: Princeton University Press, 2005.

Lee, Sang Hyun, and Allen C. Guelzo, eds. *Edwards in Our Time: Jonathan Edwards and the Shaping of American Religion*. Grand Rapids: Wm. B. Eerdmans, 1999.

Lesser, M. X. *Reading Jonathan Edwards: An Annotated Bibliography in Three Parts, 1729–2005*. Grand Rapids: Wm. B. Eerdmans, 2007.

For Further Reading

Marsden, George M. *Jonathan Edwards: A Life*. New Haven: Yale University Press, 2003.

McClymond, Michael. *Encounters with God: An Approach to the Theology of Jonathan Edwards*. New York: Oxford University Press, 1998.

McClymond, Michael James. *Encyclopedia of Religious Revivals in America*. 2 vols. Westport, CT: Greenwood Press, 2007.

McDermott, Gerald R. "Jonathan Edwards and the American Indians: The Devil Sucks Their Blood." *The New England Quarterly* 72, no. 4 (December 1999): 539–57.

———. *Jonathan Edwards Confronts the Gods: Christian Theology, Enlightenment Religion, and Non-Christian Faiths*. New York: Oxford University Press, 2000.

Miller, Perry. *Jonathan Edwards*. New York: William Sloane, 1949.

———. *The New England Mind: The Seventeenth Century*. Cambridge, MA: Harvard University Press, 1954.

Minkema, Kenneth P. "Jonathan Edwards's Defense of Slavery." *The Massachusetts Historical Review* 4 (2002): 23–59.

———. "Jonathan Edwards in the Twentieth Century." *Journal of the Evangelical Theological Society* 47, no. 4 (2004): 659–87.

———. "Old Age and Religion in the Writings and Life of Jonathan Edwards." *Church History* 70, no. 4 (December 2001): 674–704.

Minkema, Kenneth, and Harry Stout. "The Edwardsean Tradition and the Antislavery Debate, 1740–1865." *Journal of American History* 92, no. 1 (June 2005): 47–74.

Moody, Josh. *Jonathan Edwards and the Enlightenment: Knowing the Presence of God*. Lanham, MD: University Press of America, 2005.

Niebuhr, Helmut Richard. *The Kingdom of God in America*, with a new introduction by Martin Marty. Middleton, CT: Wesleyan University Press, 1988.

Noll, Mark A. *America's God: From Jonathan Edwards to Abraham Lincoln*. New York: Oxford University Press, 2002.

Pauw, Amy Plantinga. *"The Supreme Harmony of All": The Trinitarian Theology of Jonathan Edwards*. Grand Rapids: Wm. B. Eerdmans, 2002.

For Further Reading

Piper, John, and Justin Taylor, eds. *A God-Entranced Vision of All Things: The Legacy of Jonathan Edwards.* Wheaton, IL: Crossway Books, 2004.

Schmidt, Leigh. "The Edwards Revival: Or, the Public Consequences of Exceedingly Careful Scholarship." *The William and Mary Quarterly* 3rd ser., 58, no. 2 (April 2001): 480–86.

Smith, John Edwin. *Jonathan Edwards: Puritan, Preacher, Philosopher.* Notre Dame, IN: University of Notre Dame Press, 1992.

Stein, Stephen J., ed. *The Cambridge Companion to Jonathan Edwards.* Cambridge: Cambridge University Press, 2007.

———. *Jonathan Edwards's Writings: Text, Context, Interpretation.* Bloomington: Indiana University Press, 1996.

Stout, Harry S. *The New England Soul: Preaching and Religious Culture in Colonial New England.* New York: Oxford University Press, 1986.

Stout, Harry S., Kenneth P. Minkema, and Caleb J. D. Maskell. *Jonathan Edwards at 300: Essays on the Tercentenary of His Birth.* Lanham, MD: University Press of America, 2005.

Sweeney, Douglas A. *Nathaniel Taylor, New Haven Theology, and the Legacy of Jonathan Edwards.* New York: Oxford University Press, 2003.

Sweeney, Douglas A., and Allen C. Guelzo. *The New England Theology: From Jonathan Edwards to Edwards Amasa Park.* Grand Rapids: Baker Academic, 2006.

Tracy, Patricia J. *Jonathan Edwards, Pastor: Religion and Society in Eighteenth Century Northampton.* New York: Hill & Wang, 1980.

Wheeler, Rachel. "'Friends to Your Souls': Jonathan Edwards' Indian Pastorate and the Doctrine of Original Sin." *Church History* 72, no. 4 (December 2003): 736–65.

Winiarski, Douglas. "Jonathan Edwards, Enthusiast? Radical Revivalism and the Great Awakening in the Connecticut Valley." *Church History* 74, no. 4 (December 2005): 683–739.

Zakai, Avihu. *Jonathan Edwards' Philosophy of History: The Re-Enchantment of the World in the Age of Enlightenment.* New York: Routledge & Kegan Paul, 2001.

Index

affections, 48–50,
    51, 93, 111,
    139, 173
    defined, 48–50
    See also *Treatise
    Concerning
    Religious
    Affections*
African Americans,
    40
Anglican, 45, 83
Arminianism, 39–40,
    76, 80–85,
    91–102, 158,
    163, 165
Arminius, Jacobus,
    80

baptism, 68
Baptist, xii, 157,
    163, 165, 171
Barth, Karl, 167
Bartlett, Phoebe, 42
beauty, xii, 1, 15, 18,
    24, 25–30, 36,
    55, 129–30, 133,
    136, 138–39,
    142–43
Beecher, Henry
    Ward, 160
Beecher, Lyman,
    158–61
Bellamy, Joseph, 151

Bible
    and covenant the-
    ology, 121–22
    as moral standard,
    9–11, 99
    and nature,
    15–19, 24–25
    and original sin,
    111
    and religious
    experience,
    53–54
    and slavery,
    152–53
    typological inter-
    pretation of,
    17–20
    See also New Tes-
    tament, Old
    Testament
Brainerd, David, 74,
    165–66
Brown, John,
    154–55
Burr, Aaron, 147
Burr, Aaron, Jr.,
    158–59
Burr, Esther
    Edwards, 147

Calvin, John, 40, 78,
    168
Calvinism, 3, 76, 78,

    84, 97, 104–5,
    129, 131, 151,
    157–58, 160,
    166–68, 171
Cane Ridge, revival
    at, 163
Catholicism. *See*
    Roman Catholic
    Church
Chauncy, Charles, 57
children, 18, 68
    and anxieties over
    salvation, 42
    of Jonathan
    and Sarah
    Edwards, 149
Christ. *See* Jesus
    Christ
Chubb, Thomas, 83
College of New Jer-
    sey (Princeton),
    147
communion contro-
    versy in
    Northampton,
    66–73, 108–10,
    162–63
conscience, 141–43
conversion, 5–6, 39,
    41, 52–56, 67,
    71, 146
covenant, 117,
    121–22

Index

Cutler, Timothy, 80

Davenport, James, 46–47, 51, 57
death, 40–42
    of Christ (and atonement), 20
    of Edwards, 102, 149, 151, 157, 161
Declaration of Independence, 77–78
deism, 10, 24, 25, 83, 158
devil. *See* Satan/devil(s)
Distinguishing Marks of a Work of the Spirit of God, 47
Divine and Supernatural Light, 31
dueling, 158–59
Dwight, Timothy, 158, 160

Edwards, Esther Stoddard, 3
Edwards, Jerusha, 74
Edwards, Jonathan
    childhood of, 1–2, 3–5
    death of, 149
    diary of, 10
    dismissal from Northampton pastorate, 61–76
    legacy of, 147–73
    ministerial training of, 3–6, 9
    missionary work of, 73–76, 165

pastoral ministry of, 61–76, 108–9
    personality of, 2, 9, 148
    and personal morality, 10
    physical description of, 2, 148
    and Sarah Pierpont Edwards, 29–30
    scholarly vocation of, 148–149
    and spiritual anxieties of, 2, 5, 9, 10
Edwards, Jonathan, Jr., 151
Edwards, Sarah Pierpont, 29–30, 149–50
Edwards, Timothy, 3–6
election, 26, 52
End for Which God Created the World, 13–14, 127–33, 171
England, 66, 74–75, 80, 82–83, 105
Enlightenment, xiii, 3, 21–25, 77–78, 103–4, 127, 133, 171
Erskine, John, 100
ethics and morality, xiii, 56–58, 83–84, 88, 95–99, 125, 130, 133–46, 173. *See also* moral philosophy
evangelicalism, 157, 163–66, 169–73

evil, xiii, 20–21, 25, 41, 44, 59, 78–79, 90, 96–98, 101, 103–4, 110, 112–13, 117, 119–20, 122, 125, 142–43, 151–52, 154, 158. *See also*, Satan/devil(s)
excellency, 27, 28, 31

Faithful Narrative of the Surprising Work of God, 38–40, 43, 164
Finney, Charles, xii, 43, 161–63
First Amendment, 159
France, 66, 74
Franklin, Benjamin, 10–13, 77, 134–35
Freedom of the Will, 83–102, 104, 105, 116, 127, 149, 166, 169

God
    beauty of, 138–39, 143
    continuous creation of, 123–24
    delight in, 25–26
    excellency of, 26–27
    glory of in creation, 128–33
    and the problem of evil, 78–79, 103, 117–21

Index

as revealed in
nature, 13–21
sovereignty of,
24–25, 78–80,
100, 168
as Trinity, 27,
139–40
as ultimate being,
137–38
God Glorified, 81
grace, 27, 36, 56,
69–70, 81–82,
102
Graham, Billy, xii,
43, 155–56
Great Awakening, xii,
33, 35–59. *See
also* revival, Sec-
ond Great Awak-
ening

Half Way Covenant,
68
Harvard, 8, 81, 168
heaven, 28–29, 40,
56, 58
hell, xi, 2, 25, 28,
35–36, 40, 42,
58, 110, 154
*History of the Work of
Redemption*, 58,
149
Hobbes, Thomas,
19
Holy Spirit, 51, 53,
55, 119, 140
Hopkins, Samuel,
151–55
Howe, Julia Ward,
and *Battle Hymn
of the Republic*,
154
*Humble Inquiry into
the Rules of the*

Word of God, 70,
73
Hutcheson, Francis,
136–37
Hutchinson, Abigail,
41–42

idealism, 25
*Images of Divine
Things* (also *Shad-
ows of Divine
Things*), 18, 130
inclination, 49, 85,
87–88, 93, 99,
101, 112

Jefferson, Thomas,
77–78
Jesuits, 74–75
Jesus Christ, 27, 29,
31, 56, 58,
66, 82, 97,
108, 110, 112,
165, 168
moral example of,
11
types of, 17, 19–20
Judaism, 10
justification by faith,
39–40

liberalism, 8, 166–68
*Life of David Brain-
erd*, 74, 165–66
Locke, John, 3
Luther, Martin, 40

Manly, Basil, Jr., 165
Marsden, George, 170
Massachusetts Bay
Colony, 67
Mather, Cotton, 22
Methodist, xii, 82,
157–58, 163–65

millennium, 58, 110
Miller, Perry, 168–70
Miscellanies, 10
missions, 73–76, 83,
108, 165–66
Mohicans, 73, 76
Moody, Dwight, xii
moral philosophy,
133–35, 139, 142
motive, 85–88, 93,
97, 99, 101, 112,
117

Native Americans, xiii
missions to,
73–76
nature, 13–14,
20–22, 24,
27–28, 129
and the Bible,
15–19, 24–25
*Nature of True
Virtue*, 127–28,
133–46
necessity, natural and
moral, 87–90
neo-orthodoxy,
166–68
New Divinity, 151,
157
New Haven Theol-
ogy, 157
New Testament, 17,
18
Matthew (7:16),
56
Romans (5:14),
17; (5:19),
116; (12:11),
41
1 Corinthians
(1:29–31), 81
1 Timothy (1:17),
26

Index

Newton, Isaac, 3, 13, 22, 24, 95
Niebuhr, H. Richard, 168
Niebuhr, Reinhold, 168–69
Northampton, Massachusetts
  Edwards's dismissal from, 61–76, 108–10
  Edwards's early ministry in, 18, 32
  Edwards's family history in, 3
  and revivals during Edwards's pastorate, 38–39, 44
  Solomon Stoddard's ministry in, 32, 66–73

Old Testament: 17
  Genesis (2–3), 116
  Job, 42
Original Sin, 105–26, 127, 149

Parrington, Vernon, 166
passions, 48, 51, 55, 57
Personal Narrative, 5, 26, 164
philosophy, xii, 3, 25, 27–28, 99, 136–37, 166, 171–72.
Piper, John, 171–72
pornography, 63

preaching, 5, 7, 66–67
Presbyterian, 2, 9, 105
psychology, 37, 40, 84, 169
Puritanism, xiii, 6–7, 10, 168
  importance of preaching in, 7
  and missions, 75
  and standards of church membership, 66–73

reason, xiii, 11, 21, 31, 76, 84, 111
religious affections. *See* affections, *Treatise Concerning Religious Affections*
Resolutions, 11–12, 164
revival, xii, 5, 31–32, 33, 35–59, 61–62, 65, 82, 85, 146, 170–71
  in camp meetings, 163
  and controversy, 38, 43, 45–47, 52, 57, 59, 161–62
  and Edwards's legacy, 155–66
  and "new measures," 161–62
  in world history, 38–39, 58
Revolutionary War, xii, 78

Roman Catholic Church, 74–75, 134
Root, Simeon, 62–65
Root, Timothy, 62–65

sacraments, 32
Satan/devil(s), 6, 20, 21, 23, 44, 48, 52–53, 55, 66, 110, 117, 143
science, 3, 10, 13, 149, 169
  conversion as, 69
  Edwards's interest in, 13–15, 21–22, 40, 149
  revival as, 43, 161
Scopes Trial, 21
Scotland, 73, 100
Scripture. *See* Bible
Second Great Awakening, 157–58, 160
sermons, xi, 7, 31–32, 35–37, 40, 46–47, 58, 64–65, 73–75, 124, 128, 149, 154–55, 159, 169, 171
sexuality, 62
sin, xiii, 5, 12, 41, 44, 76, 80–82, 84, 90, 101–2, 103–26, 127, 143, 157–58, 161, 168
"Sinners in the Hands of an Angry God," xi, xii, xiii, 35–36, 38, 42, 124, 154–55

slavery, 151–55, 157, 160
smallpox, 149
Southern Baptist Theological Seminary, 165, 171
Spider Letter, 13, 14, 29
spiders, xii, 13, 15, 124, 129
Stockbridge mission, 73
Stoddard, John, 72–73
Stoddard, Solomon, 3, 32–33, 68–72, 75, 109, 162
Stout, Harry, 35
Stowe, Harriet Beecher, 160
and *Uncle Tom's Cabin*, 160
suicide, 44–45

Taylor, John, 105–13
Taylor, Nathaniel William, 160–61
Ten Commandments, 99, 113

Treatise Concerning Religious Affections, 47–58, 62, 85, 93, 146, 164, 171
Trinity Evangelical Divinity School, 171
Types of the Messiah, 18

United States, 77, 150

virtue, 125–26, 127–46

war, xii, xiii, 66, 74–75, 134, 167
and preaching, 7
Warner, Oliver, 62
Watts, Isaac, 83, 92–93
Wesley, Charles, 5, 45
Wesley, John, 5, 38, 45, 165
Whitby, Daniel, 83

Whitefield, George, xii, 37, 45–46, 61, 156–57
will, 50, 76, 77–102, 112
Edwards's definition of, 85, 92–93
Williams, Solomon, 109
witchcraft, 22–23
women
in Edwards's writings, 5, 41–42
as spiritual and theological influences on Edwards, 4–5, 29–30
as victims of harassment, 63

Yale, 2, 80, 158, 160
and Edwards's education, 8
and *Works of Jonathan Edwards*, 169–70